THE THIRD JOB

The Third Job

Employed couples' management of household
work contradictions

Gurjeet K. Gill
Department of Social Anthropology
Massey University,
New Zealand

 Routledge
Taylor & Francis Group

LONDON AND NEW YORK

First published 1998 by Ashgate Publishing

Reissued 2018 by Routledge
2 Park Square, Milton Park, Abingdon, Oxon OX14 4RN
52 Vanderbilt Avenue, New York, NY 10017

Routledge is an imprint of the Taylor & Francis Group, an informa business

Publisher's Note
The publisher has gone to great lengths to ensure the quality of this reprint but points out that some imperfections in the original copies may be apparent.

Disclaimer
The publisher has made every effort to trace copyright holders and welcomes correspondence from those they have been unable to contact.

A Library of Congress record exists under LC control number: 98071964

ISBN 13: 978-1-138-32303-2 (hbk)
ISBN 13: 978-0-429-42957-6 (ebk)

Contents

List of Figures   *vi*
List of Tables   *vii*
Preface   *ix*
Acknowledgements   *xi*

1   Assessment of Household Work Contradictions   1

2   Solutions to Contradictions over Household Work   11

3   Conceptual Framework and Central Claim   21

4   Research Philosophy and Methodology   39

5   How Do Families Handle External and Internal
    Constraints?   55

6   How Do Women Handle Personal Goals, Role
    Definitions and Dilemmas?   80

7   Are the Perceptions of Ground Rules
    and of Self and Other, Flexible or Inflexible?   106

8   Effective Management Versus Household Crisis   140

9   Is the Style of Household Management Flexible
    or Rigid?   165

10 Managing Household Work Contradictions   191

    Bibliography   200

    Index   210

List of Figures

3.1 Loose coupling between the institutional order
and the interaction order   34

3.2 Loose coupling between the institutional order and the
family interaction order   36

3.3 Typology of rules in the family interaction order   38

9.1 Negotiation of household work in three-job families   181

List of Tables

4.1 Families Interviewed   44

4.2 Age of Husbands and Wives   45

4.3 Educational Status of Husbands and Wives   45

4.4 Occupational Status of Husbands and Wives   45

4.5 Employment (hours/week) of Husbands and Wives   46

4.6 Earnings ($/week) of Husbands and Wives   46

4.7 Religious Background of Husbands and Wives   46

4.8 Distribution of Trade-off and Rigid Rules According
    to Family Models   53

5.1 Perceived Constraints/ (Means) and Ends   56

6.1 Personal Goals, Role Definitions and Source
    of Knowledge   81

7.1 Husband's Perceptions of Self/Identity,
    Own Roles, Partner's Identity, Partner's Roles,
    and Negotiation Pattern   107

7.2 Wife's Perceptions of Self/Identity, Own Roles,
    Partner's Identity, Partner's Roles, and Negotiation
    Pattern   111

8.1 Redefinition of Family Order, Quality of Interaction
     and Household Management Style   141

9.1 Family Interaction Style and Coping Strategies   166

Preface

This book is about three-job (two-paid and one household work) families. It is about couples who are involved in the labour market and face the enormous task of unpaid 'third job' of managing their households. Here, the third job of 'household management' is perceived as a 'job' in its own right. At a general level, it is unpaid and gender specific and includes the performance of household work and child-care activities, decision-making, worrying, planning, negotiating and the designing of coping strategies, as well as any other activity considered important for the overall family management. However, more specifically it is conceptualised at two levels: ideological and practical. In the ideological sense it is the running of household affairs to carry out a 'normal' family life (Brennan and Moss, 1991: 2), and in the practical sense it is the performance of household work 'necessary' for the sustenance of family members. The two aspects are interlinked as they both implicate one another.

Because both partners are involved in the labour market they lack essential resources (time, energy) to do the required household work in order to manage their families. They also lack a sense of 'sharedness' towards the responsibility of household work that mainly implicates women. Ideally when both partners are involved in the paid work they should share the household work. This is not as simple as it seems. The backdrop (family role-relationship, gender ideology, patriarchy, socialisation) at which the division of household labour is negotiated and carried out by couples, is in contradiction with the three-job family situation. By this I mean the labour market, to which couples are contracted to, bears contradictions that mostly implicate wives and mothers. For example, within the macro institutional order (labour market) some aspects such as Equal Employment Opportunity and Affirmative Action are contradicted by a lack of child-care, patriarchy and rigid job structure. Similarly within family (micro interaction order) managing the household work requires adaptation and readjustment of household division of labour which may be in contradiction with the traditional images of husbands and wives. Consequently contradictory features within and between the labour market and the family lead to household work contradictions.

Household work contradictions are acutely experienced in the everyday life of three-job families. In order to manage household work contradictions the couples in three-job families devise household management rules as strategies and tactics. The effective or ineffective management of household work contradictions lies in the nature of household management rules. Five such rules (in Chapters 5-9) are used to describe the process by which families (under two models: Trade-off and Rigid) manage household work contradictions either effectively or ineffectively. Families under the Trade-off Model manage household work judiciously and effectively whereas families under the Rigid Model manage household work contradictions chaotically and ineffectively.

Theoretical increment in this book is the graphical specification of the relationship of macro institutional order (labour market) and micro interaction order (family). This is done through 'loose coupling' as an attempt to overcome the macro-micro dualism by envisaging individuals and society as inseparable and indivisible.

This book acts as a window into the everyday lives of households in which employed couples struggle with the 'third job' of household work in order to keep their families together. It is about their discourse on the ways in which they handle constraints, how women as wives and mothers handle personal goals, role definitions and dilemmas, whether they negotiate ground rules or not to suit their three-job family situation, whether they manage their three-job families effectively or run into household crisis, and whether they use flexible or inflexible style to manage their households.

Acknowledgements

I am grateful to the three-job families who welcomed me into their households and gave me their time and talked freely about their households.

This book has evolved from a doctoral dissertation written under the supervision of Peter Lucich in the Department of Sociology at the University of New England, Australia. I wish to acknowledge his invaluable advice, constructive criticism and patience. My gratitude is due to Hugh Potter and Jim Bell for their helpful suggestions and their encouragement. I am grateful to Michael Bittman, Jacqueline Goodnow, Jane Hood and Betsy Wearing for providing valuable critical comments on the thesis version of this book.

I am grateful to Mary-Helen Ward for proof-reading the script promptly and patiently. My gratitude is also due to Heather Hodgetts for preparing the camera-ready copy. I couldn't have done it without her help.

I am thankful to the Department of Social Anthropology, Massey University for providing ideal environment for the production of this book.

I am fortunate to have had the support of my family, friends, and colleagues that kept my enthusiasm during the preparation of this book. I am very grateful to Celia Briar for her motivation and support. I am specially thankful to Catherine Brennan for encouraging me to publish this book.

Thanks are also due to my publisher, Ashgate, for providing the opportunity to share three-job families, experience of household management with readers.

To my children, Navraj and Preet, and to my husband, Harsharn, for their unconditional love, encouragement and forbearance, I dedicate this book.

1 Assessment of Household Work Contradictions

Rapid changes in society over recent years, particularly the increasing number of families in which both partners work in the labour market, have led to changes in family structures in Australia. Women's labour force participation has been on the increase since the 1960s. In 1966 women's labour force participation rate was 30 per cent of the Australian work force (Women's Bureau, 1968: 11). It increased to 41.8 per cent in 1991 (Women's Bureau, 1991: 12) and 52.9 per cent in 1996 (Australian Bureau of Statistics, 1996b: 6-8). Similarly, married women's labour force participation has increased from 12 per cent (O'Donnell and Hall, 1988: 7) in the early 1950s to 52.5 per cent in 1996 (Australian Bureau of Statistics, 1996b). Recent changes in the labour market and equal opportunity provisions, together with the International Labour Organisation convention 156, have helped women to move into and stay in the labour market (Office for the Status of Women, 1992: 3). In conjunction with the Australian government's commitment to the International Labour Organisation convention, a policy is in place that entitles both mothers and fathers to parental leave. To further facilitate women's labour market involvement, the Office for Status of Women is committed to making structural changes in the domestic division of labour and to increasing men's contribution to housework (Bittman, 1991). These facts indicate a favourable trend in the macro institutional order that facilitates women's involvement in the economy.

On the other hand, women's role in the labour market is considered as secondary and in addition to their institutionalised roles in the domestic sphere, as they often favour part-time employment and choose to drop out of the work force during child-bearing years (Evans, 1991: 147-159). This is because household work is still considered to be

1

women's work even as people's perceptions change. Bittman and Lovejoy (1993) describe an overt disjunction between belief and action, as there is now a broad subscription to the 'new' values of gender equity (Holmstrom, 1985: 4), yet a 'traditional' sexual division of labour still persists (Bittman, 1991). This discrepancy can be described as 'pseudomutuality' (Wynne, Ryckoff, Day and Hirsh, 1967: 444). Bittman and Pixely (1997: 145-171) discussed pseudomutuality in the context of domestic division of labour. They argued that strong commitment to the value of equality and companionship in intimate relations is combined with the inability to live out these principles. This results in situation where it is difficult for either partner to acknowledge the inequalities in the relationship. They further affirm that couples' commitment to an equal, pure relationship barely hides the apparent relations of power and the result is frustration, guilt and pain.

Even when employed women reduce their domestic labour considerably, especially if they are employed for more than 30 hours per week they still do more household work than men (Bittman, 1991: 21). Although some fathers are sharing parenting responsibilities (Russell, 1983), it is women who feel guilty for using substitute child-care (Shaw and Burns, 1993: 30-43). This shows that although favourable changes are taking place at the macro institutional level, similar results are yet to be achieved in the micro interaction order.

Equity for women in the labour market and in Equal Opportunity legislation on the one hand, and expectations of traditional family roles on the other, have produced and exacerbated contradictions inside the family. These contradictions have to be dealt with both by families and by social theorists of family and gender.

Accordingly, the main question explored in this book is *who manages the household when husband and wife are involved in the labour market?* In other words, who will take the responsibility? Here, the third job of 'household management' is perceived as a 'job' in its own right. At a general level, it is unpaid and gender specific and includes the performance of household work and child-care activities, decision-making, worrying, planning, negotiating and the designing of coping strategies, as well as any other activity considered important for the overall family management. However, more specifically it is conceptualised at two levels: ideological and practical. In the ideological sense it is the running of household affairs to carry out a 'normal family life' (Brennan and Moss, 1991: 2), and in the practical sense it is the

2

performance of household work 'necessary' for the sustenance of family members. The two aspects are interlinked as they both implicate one another.

The household work contradictions involved can be illustrated from discrepancies within and between macro institutional and micro interaction orders that cause problems for three-job (two paid and one household work) families. For example, within the macro institutional order (labour market) some aspects such as Equal Employment Opportunity and Affirmative Action are contradicted by a lack of child-care and rigid job structures, as well as patriarchy, that mostly implicate women workers. Contradictions between macro and micro orders result, because typification, schema, cultural traditions in the macro institutional order regarding men and women and their family roles may conflict with the need for sense of identity and with the need to adjust, adapt and co-operate in the family interaction order. Similarly within the micro interaction order (family) the need to adapt and adjust to a three-job family way of life maybe in contradiction with the prevailing images of self/other and family roles of men and women as husbands and wives, and fathers and mothers respectively. Household work contradictions become real issues for working couples, because these act as obstacles (ideological or practical, material or institutional, personal or social) that encumber the workings of three-job households.

Given that household work contradictions are acutely experienced in daily interactions within three-job families, I will argue that in order to solve those problems, families devise their own interaction orders. I further contend that household work contradictions can be relatively effectively managed by means of devising specific sets of household management rules in the interaction order.

The significance of the question is both moral and theoretical. The moral issues relate to autonomy and equity. The theoretical significance is in the articulation of the conflicting institutional demands with the as yet un-institutionalised practices at the face to face and interpersonal level. In other words, three-job families have to continually negotiate rules and invent strategies to deal with contradicting features within and between the macro institutional order and micro interaction order. The value of studying these issues lies in the enhanced understanding of the obstacles encountered by three-job couples in managing their families. By understanding these obstacles it maybe possible for some of the constraints to be reduced or even entirely eliminated.

In Chapter 2, I review relevant literature to find solutions to household work contradictions. In Chapter 3, I discuss a conceptual framework, considering both macro institutional order and micro interaction order, to graphically show how household work contradictions implicate three-job families. Chapter 4 describes research philosophy and methods used in the study on which this book is based. Chapters 5-9 specify the ways in which families deal with the third job in order to manage household work contradictions. In this chapter, I will first establish the increasing presence of household work contradictions in families in which both partners are employed. Secondly, I will discuss how household work has come to be defined as a 'job'.

Household work contradictions are increasing

Significant changes have taken place in the patterns of employment and unemployment in Australia since 1980. Although all women's participation in the labour force has increased markedly (52.9 per cent) the rate of increase of married women's participation (52.5 per cent) in employment is substantial (Australian Bureau of Statistics, 1996b: 6-8).

Simultaneous changes in welfare policies may have enhanced women's capacity to enter and stay in the labour force. Until the early 1980s women were perceived as 'legitimate dependants' for welfare purposes (Bryson, 1983). However, during the mid-eighties a change in policy made most entitlements gender neutral. The widow's pension was abolished and efforts were made to direct women who were social security recipients into the labour force (Bryson, 1993: 72). The Australian federal government announced the JET scheme (Jobs, Education and Training) for sole parents in the 1988 Budget. This was a job training programme especially aimed at women (Colledge, 1991: 31).

The Australian government has also made explicit commitments to fostering equality between women and men within families and bringing about a fuller sharing of domestic responsibilities and employment opportunities (Office for the Status of Women, 1992: 3). In contrast, as far as the family domain is concerned, domestic responsibilities have largely remained women's work. Bittman found that over a period of 13 years (between 1974 and 1987) women had reduced their time spent in housework by 4 hours per week, while men had increased their time by

4

2 hours and 21 minutes (Bittman, 1991: 21). He suggests that even though employed women are reducing their unpaid hours in the domestic sphere, a husband's contribution to housework has only increased by about one hour per week, whether his wife is working 10 or 40 hours (Bittman, 1991: 21).

Bittman and Lovejoy (1993) suggest a contradiction between 'belief' and 'action', or an ethos of equity and a reality of inequality regarding domestic division of labour in families. I think this is a valuable concept in understanding domestic power and the processes of negotiation, allocation and performance of household work in families.

The existing gender-based division of domestic labour within the three-job families can be seen as a result of contradicting features within and between the macro and micro orders of the society. For example, in three-job families contradiction emerges between the need for a flexible re-arrangement of household work and an attachment to traditional divisions and standards. As a result, women find themselves under pressure to bear the responsibility of managing the household in addition to their paid work. This indicates that the unpaid 'job' of household work becomes problematic. It is a problem mainly because the families in the interaction order still work within the framework of a traditional division of labour. Consequently, women bear the household responsibility with fewer resources (time, energy, and money for adequate paid help in household) at hand. Although Equal Opportunity and Affirmative Action in the institutional order have enhanced women's representation in the labour market, adequate and accessible child-care and paid parental leave is still a problem for many working mothers. Similarly, there is a discrepancy between men's and women's earnings that reflects the patriarchal wage structure in the institutional order (Bryson, 1993). Arber and Ginn (1995: 40) describe a reciprocal relationship between women's economic disadvantage in the labour market and their domestic role in the family, which in turn limits their full potential in the public sphere.

Similar contradictions have been reported by family researchers who turned to measure household task performance. Several large scale overseas studies (Berk and Berk, 1979; Szalai, 1972; Walker and Woods, 1976; Vanek, 1980) reported that women bear the burden of household work. Walker and Woods (1976: 44) found that whether women participated in the labour force or not, they performed more housework than their husbands. They also found that young children's

5

presence in the home increased a mother's time spent on housework compared to a father's. This leads to a time availability theory, which claims that a couple's time spent in the housework is taken as relative to their time in the labour market. Some studies report that a husband's participation in household labour is related to a wife's participation in paid work (Huber and Spitze, 1983; Pleck, 1985; Coverman, 1985; Presland and Antill, 1987). However, other research has reported no relationship between household division of labour and a couple's time spent in the labour market (Stafford, Backman and Dibona, 1977; Ross, 1987).

Researchers have also focused on sex role attitudes and their effect on the household division of labour. They have attempted to measure sex role attitudes using structured questionnaires on men's and women's gender roles and role reversal (Pleck, 1985; Coverman, 1985). Although sex role attitudes have contributed much to the understanding of husband-wife relationships, one cannot isolate them from other variables such as class, education, and so forth. Education as a predictor had been studied by Farkas (1976) and Geerkon and Gove (1983). Their results suggest that educational attainment is directly related to egalitarian sex role attitudes. This maybe contradicted from the relative resource theoretical perspective which explains that the spouse with higher level of education has more power to negotiate and consequently may do less housework. Thompson and Walker (1989: 856-867) concluded that 'there is no simple trade-off of wage and family work hours between husbands and wives, nor do partners allocate family work on time-availability.'

Recent research on task allocation and its performance shows that women would rather take on a disproportionate share of housework to avoid conflict than pressure their husbands to contribute more to household work (Berheide, 1984; Hochschild, 1989). Shaw (1988: 333-337) suggested that housework, as caring for other family members, is taken to be an essential part of women's identity, and therefore any conflict over caring for family members maybe interpreted by others as not caring about family members (cf. Able and Nelson, 1990).

Mederer (1993) conceptualised household labour not only as accomplishing tasks, but also as defining them as necessary, creating standards for their performance, and making sure that they are done in an acceptable manner. She surveyed 359 married full-time employed women to test the extent to which task accomplishment versus household management predict perceptions of fairness and conflict. Mederer suggested that when household labour allocation is considered as an independent variable it becomes part of the micro interaction in the family, and implies connections with the macro structure of gender inequality. She found a significant relationship between housework allocation and perceptions of fairness. She also reported 'the more housework women in my sample did, and the more time they spent doing it relative to their husbands, the more conflict they reported' (Mederer, 1993: 142). She further argued that task accomplishment and family life management are different dimensions of family work, and each dimension contributes separately to perceptions of family work.

In time-budget research, two studies by Berk and Berk (1979) and Berk (1985) showed that women are still doing 96 per cent of the cooking, 92 per cent of the dish-washing, 90 per cent of the vacuuming, 94 per cent of the bed-making and 94 per cent of the nappy changing as part of child-care. In their earlier survey, Walker and Woods (1976) found that unemployed women spent a higher percentage of total time in housework performance than men. However, they also showed that employed women still carried out the household burden, with only a minor increase in the time spent by their husbands (Walker and Woods, 1976: 45).

In general the overseas and Australian literature on the quantification of household task performance indicates inequalities of task performance between men and women, even when women are employed. Research on household division of labour discussed earlier in this chapter confirms household work contradictions and claims that unequal relations exist in the household division of labour even when both partners are involved in paid work. This draws our attention to the argument presented earlier that there is a conflict over household labour in three job/two earner families. It is a result of contradicting features within and between the macro institutional order and the micro interaction order that merge when women combine paid work and family responsibilities. For example, some of the structures in the macro institutional order such as equal opportunity, gender role orientation, job structure are contradictory as well as incompatible with the needs and resources of the modern family in which both partners are employed. In other words, although efforts of equal opportunity are being made in the macro institutional order and women are entering the labour market in large numbers, the corresponding changes have not yet taken place in the workings of families in which both partners are in the labour force. Similarly, the traditional division of labour, family roles and the identity need of individuals in families are now incompatible with the institutional structures of the society. As a result, there are increasing household work contradictions which the couples in three-job families have to address and resolve. This is problematic not only for families in which both partners are employed but for theorists of gender, family and general social theory.

Perceptions of household work are changing

Influenced by women's movements in the 1960s and 1970s, researchers began to examine women's position in the family and to question the notion of companionship in marriage. Friedan (1963) perceived women as prisoners in the family home. This was further supported by Gavron (1983), who highlighted the socially constructed meaning of paid and unpaid work from a study of 96 London housewives, and argued that women have the choice to work or to stay at home. Staying at home, however, does not involve equal recognition, even if women are spending twice as much time doing the housework. She further examined the impact of technology on household tasks, and she concluded that it had increased both the actual time and expectations to meet the standards of ideal housewives and successful career women (Gavron, 1983: 127-128). In other words, signs of gender inequality began to appear in the analysis of men's and women's family roles, which indicated the need for a recognition of work done by wives.

Oakley (1974: 24-25) attempted to overcome the invisibility of women in sociology, by examining the nature of housework. Her prime concern was to conceptualise housework as work, rather than simply as an aspect of the feminine role in marriage (Oakley, 1974: 181-182). She argued that society assigns role definitions to men and women in terms of their paid work, and in this sense men are seen to do the 'real' work. Women do not, since housework is not defined as work (Oakley, 1974: 25). Her study was based on interviews with 40 housewives revealing their attitudes and perceptions of satisfaction and dissatisfaction with housework chores. In studying their husbands' participation, she concluded that only a few husbands equally shared housework with their wives. Further, their participation depended upon their social class

8

position, and they were more involved in the child-care tasks than the menial chores. She further indicated that with women's increased labour force participation, husband's task performance increases.

Oakley (1974) also explored how women felt about their housewife role. She learned that women were not so much dissatisfied with their role as housewives as with their chores which were monotonous, boring, and repetitive. Oakley believed that gender socialisation defined women as housewives and mothers and therefore they feel pressured to be 'good housewives and mothers.' Although Oakley has made a significant contribution to sociologists' knowledge of housework, her research is not without problems. The used to study housework and industrial work maybe problematic. Smith (1979) argued that the concepts used to study the relations between bourgeoisie and proletariat may not be adequate to study the social relations between husband and wife. In other words, household activities such as caring for others (husband and children) cannot be perceived as similar to proletarian work for the capitalist. As Game and Pringle (1983: 126-128) argue, housework is not only the performance of several chores, it is also an important part of women's identity.

Lopata (1971) studied women's many roles, and identified the various demands on them and their ability to cope with them. She also pointed out that although some women dislike housework, many find it to be creative and autonomous. She illuminated the contradictory aspects of being a mother 'tied down' by the responsibilities of children, versus the freedom of working unsupervised as a housewife. What I am suggesting here is that housewife and mother roles are imposed by the macro structural patterns of society, and therefore women still carry out the responsibility of household management in addition to their paid work commitments. In other words, unlike men, when married women work outside the family home they are still responsible for household management.

Sharpe (1984) explained this through sex role socialisation which requires men and women to perform specific household tasks. She argued that men tend to see their homes as places to return to and to recuperate from the harsh working conditions of their employment (Sharpe, 1984: 179-180). She further argued that men who undertake housework or child-care maybe risking their masculine image and be seen as slipping into a domestic trap (Sharpe, 1984: 181). She also made an interesting suggestion about women's resistance to men sharing housework. She described this apprehension on women's part to protect their identity as providing 'a clearly marked area of responsibility carrying certain elements of power, however limited, and a definite sense of control' (Sharpe, 1984: 183). Analogous to this is women's strategy to work part-time and combine family responsibilities (Sharpe, 1984: 186-188).

Lopata, Oakley and Sharpe opened up a whole new area of research on women's role relations with other members of the family. They highlighted the need to study housework as work performed by women. However, their studies have methodological problems. Their sample consists of only women respondents presenting one side of the story, and this raises questions concerning the validity of the data. Nevertheless the outcome has been changes in the way contemporary sociologists perceive housework. The definition of 'work' has been expanded to include housework and child-care (Gauger, 1973; Gavron, 1983; Hill, 1985; Lopata, 1971; Luxton, 1980; Oakley, 1974; Vanek, 1980). A corresponding change in the conception of 'the family' has also been recognised, as the focus has shifted from the family as a unit to the individuals within a household who create a division of labour, either through conflict or negotiation (Shelton, 1992).

For these reasons couples in the present study are perceived to be managing household work as the third job in addition to their two paid jobs. From the point of view of three-job families themselves such perceptions remain private and un-institutionalised, and hidden in household work contradictions.

2 Solutions to Contradictions over Household Work

In Chapter 1, contradicting features within and between the macro institutional order/labour market and the micro interaction order/family have been identified to be the main reason for contradictions over household work in three-job families. This poses a problem that requires a solution. This chapter assesses relevant literature from interactive approaches to understand how household work contradictions are addressed and what solutions are offered to the problem.

Interactive approaches and family dynamics

Much of the earlier research on family life has been influenced by concepts taken from symbolic interactionism and phenomenological sociology. According to Schutz (see in Broderson, 1964)) 'from the outset, the world of everyday life is a universe of significance to us.' This encompasses a texture of meaning which we have to interpret in order to find our bearings within it and come to terms with it. In doing so, he stated, individuals are continually engaged in constructing taken-for-granted 'course of action' types. In family, 'life is a process ongoing in a situation of actual or potential instability' (Hess and Handel, 1968: 15). Berger and Kellner (1970) suggested that marriage is an ongoing conversation and a cite of 'nomos building', in which the spouses bring different pasts and provide their 'significant other' a major subjective importance.

In the 1920s Burgess stressed the significance of members' own conceptions of family roles and the ways in which these roles are developed through interaction within the family group itself (Burgess, 1926: 3-10). Burgess, Locke and Thomas (1945: 274, 540) described

11

the 'concept' of the modern family as other than a passive recipient and transmitter of culture from one generation to the next. They redefined it as a critical and selective cultural unit which develops according to its aspirations and objectives. They also predicted the increased participation of women and of married women in the workforce.

Burgess (1947: 1-6) gave two categories that disrupt family harmony: first, a sudden change of women's status as a result of their employment and; second, a conflict among family members in the conception of their roles. What makes a situation a crisis is largely dependent upon three factors: a) the hardships of the situation; b) the resources of the family including its role structure, flexibility, and previous history with crisis; and c) the family's definition of the situation; i.e., whether the situation is perceived as a threat or not. Subsequent studies focused on interaction patterns in families with problems (Winter and Ferreira, 1969), communication patterns within the family group (Heiss, 1968), and the negotiation of meanings within the family (Handel, 1968).

Strategies and tactics

Families use different strategies to manage their households. The notion of household strategies was introduced by Pahl (1984) to refer to 'distinctive practices adopted by members of a household collectively or individually to get work done': a strategy is the household's 'particular mix of parcels'. Brennen and Moss (1991) extended the notion of strategy by distinguishing between strategies and tactics. A strategy is the broad principles and priorities applied to the management of paid work. Tactics are the detailed practices used in applying these principles and priorities.

Backett, in her study of managing parenthood and family life, discusses a variety of strategies used by mothers and fathers in the development and negotiation of parental behaviour (Backett, 1982). It is interesting to note that couples in her study used 'myths' about sharing household labour as a coping strategy to support their belief in fair division of labour (Backett, 1982: 96). She found that the 'negotiation of parenthood involved continuous possibilities for conflict and misunderstandings' that required solution. In order to cope with these contradictions and dilemmas couples used two types of mechanisms in response to two types of problematic issues. At one level a set of coping strategies were used to cope with tensions and dilemmas which couples identified as 'amenable'. At the second level a set of strategies were used to deal with issues about which the couples felt they could do little. These were perceived as 'bearable'. It was a 'repertoire of coping mechanisms' that kept them going, on which spouses tended to draw as a tactic for solving conflict and tensions (Backett, 1982: 78).

Hood studied the renegotiation of the ground rules of households in families in which the wife had returned to the labour market (Hood, 1983: 113-139). She found that husbands and wives coped with the two-job family life style by using the following strategies: 1) reduction of role overload by learning to be satisfied with dirtier houses and simpler meals; 2) coming to terms with ambiguity about the relative priorities of each spouse's work and family roles; and 3) making their wants and needs known to each other and discussing the implications of each person's wants and needs for the other's and family's well-being (Hood, 1983: 192). Hood reported that a husband whose wife has recently re-entered the work force is more likely to take on household and child-care responsibilities if the wife 'earns 30 percent or more of the household income and is defined as a co-provider' (Hood, 1983: 197). However, it is worth noting that none of the 16 couples in her study shared the housework equally and 'that even those husbands who did take on additional responsibilities tended to choose the ones they most enjoyed' (Hood, 1983: 197). This maybe because the couples did not decide to become co-providers in order to adopt an egalitarian division of labour. In becoming a two-job family 'some couples developed a more equal balance of power in their marriage and a more equal division of labour in their household. This move towards equality was an unseen and unintended consequence of becoming co-providers' (Hood, 1983: 197).

In an attempt to understand the way in which women combine family and paid work, Yeandle (1984) interviewed 64 employed mothers, tracing their movement in and out of the labour market. She found women's labour-force participation depended upon their transitions in the sequence of being unmarried, being wives, and being mothers. Their subsequent employment pattern was based on the number and age of children, and increased domestic obligations led to a decline in the status of their employment. Although women were required to supplement the family income, they had done so in order to escape the isolation of housework.

Yeandle's study on women's efforts to combine work and family

13

responsibilities is important for a number of her conclusions. First, her overwhelming impression of the marital bargaining over the question of wives' employment was that husbands held the balance of power (Yeandle, 1984: 143). Second, husbands' participation in the housework did not increase, and the responsibility of the majority of tasks still fell on women (Yeandle, 1984: 144-146). Third, women's employment was defined as secondary to their role as housewives and mothers. Consequently women's paid work was perceived in terms of finances rather than self development. Under the models of economic rationality and patriarchy, women sought their husbands' permission before entering paid work; they combined employment with family needs, and remained only contributors to the family income (Yeandle, 1984: 59-60). Consequently women devised strategies to manage the contradictions resulting from their involvement in paid work and commitment to family responsibilities. They sought help from their husbands for partially caring for children. The husbands 'kept an eye on' or 'were at hand' on a needs basis. They took help from their children either to promote a 'work ethic' or in exchange for money. They also relied on the support of other women (especially mothers and mothers-in-law). In addition they used personal strategies, for example, part-time employment, homeworking, paid child-care service, working rather long hours, and using labour-saving devices (Yeandle, 1984: 140-177).

Sharpe provides a descriptive and analytical account of strategies used by women combining paid work and family responsibilities (1984: 8). Women in her study worked for economic necessity, self-identity and self confidence. Husbands did not object if their wives' employment did not contradict their family responsibilities. In this way wives took on additional paid work for self development. Looking at husbands' participation in housework, she found that they selectively chose tasks that were enjoyable and less repetitive and boring (1984: 177). Wives tried to fit their paid work life into established domestic patterns so that there was as little disorganisation as possible in the family. Part-time work was a strategy by which women earned extra cash for the family and remained responsible for their families. In order to minimise the effect of their employment on their family life they kept their domestic spheres uninterrupted and continued as if 'they did not go out to work' (Sharpe, 1984:188). Sharpe believes that because women bend their working lives to suit the needs of domestic routines, they hinder progress towards renegotiation of housework and child-care with men. They work part-time and fit housework and child-care into their remaining 'free time' (Sharpe, 12984: 187-188).

Lien studied 23 two-parent two-earner families to examine how family members felt about their primary family responsibilities (Lein, 1984). She explored how social pressures and traditional ideology affect the family division of labour. She found that the mothers' concern for their children was not hampered by their involvement in the labour market, and she suggested that maternal employment changes the means by which parents meet their responsibilities (Lien, 1984: 17). Respondents in her study relied on a variety of social networks to meet a sudden demand, especially regarding child-care. With regard to household labour, she discovered that the families who were traditional in their orientation made no attempt to renegotiate housework, and consequently the wife took on paid work in addition to her home-making responsibilities (Lien, 1984: 42). In order to help the wife deal with the problems of combining paid work and family responsibilities, some couples negotiated the 'partners model' in which both partners shared housework responsibilities. This placed further stress on them because they had to take on the additional responsibility of continuing discussions and negotiations to work out an egalitarian system. This process was considered undesirable; it 'added to husband's and wife's work load, even if the end result was highly valued' (Lien, 1984: 52).

Hertz (1986) explored the intersection of ideology and institutional constraints that impacted on dual-career couples. She found that the ideology of equality, especially in marital roles, emerges out of common opportunities and constraints. Rather than becoming radical and trying to change existing social structures, the dual career couples reconstructed their family forms to cope with the constraints of work and to meet the American dream.

In dual-career marriage she found, the ideology of traditional family does not work, and for two careers to flourish simultaneously, issues of equality become crucial in the marriage. It is interesting to note that couples in her sample continuously tried to 'strike a balance between careers and family commitments by keeping each other in check, so that neither spouse could tip the balance in favour of his or her own career' (Hertz, 1986: 56). They established 'rules' to prevent disagreements and tensions over 'job offers' in other cities, 'power balance', 'extra dimensions' about each other, and a lack of benefits that the husbands

15

missed from the more traditional marriage. It is evident that dual-career couples in Hertz's study worked within non-traditional roles; however, they had to be vigilant not to fall into a gender-based division of household labour. Furthermore, the couples relied on good communication between themselves to reduce the stress that accompanied a corporate career. They felt the need to 'decompress' at the end of the work day (Hertz, 1986: 29-83).

An Australian study by Harper and Richards (1986) was concerned with the intersection of household tasks and women's labour force participation. They emphasised that the private/public split creates an image that pictures individuals as passive recipients of social statuses, prescribed rules, and products of the private haven. In contrast, by keeping within the interactionist tradition of thinking, they show how people 'make their worlds, work at their networks, make and remake the values dictating their placements, debate, dodge and interpret-negotiate with social values' (Harper and Richards, 1986: XV). In their research the most remarkable finding about household division of labour was the absence of agreed-on patterns of housework allocation (Harper and Richards, 1986: 188). Irrespective of women's labour force participation, class position, family income, and number of working hours there were enormous variations in the arrangements of households. Husbands' housework performance varied from minimum to as much as that of the wives whether wives were in paid employment or not (Harper and Richards, 1986: 188). They identified three types of contracts: 'old', 'new' and 'compromise'. They found that a majority of the couples worked between the 'old' and the 'new' contract. These couples were 'in a messy situation in which expectations of husbands and wives differed, causing confusion and conflict as their work commitments changed, as children's demands grew heavier or lighter, and as health and fatigue varied' (Harper and Richards, 1986: 194). Furthermore, they suggest that 'the renegotiation that occurs in the household contract depends on such a tangle of factors that to deal with them separately simplifies the issue to the point of unreality' (Harper and Richards, 1986: 217).

Coltrane (1989: 473-490) explored the household division of labour and the routine production of 'gender' (Coltrane, 1989: 473-490). Using the accounts of dual-career couples, he discussed the social construction of parenting from the formulation of 'doing gender' (West and Zimmerman, 1987: 125-51). He suggested that in order to cope with the demands of combining paid work and family responsibilities, the couples shared housework and parenting. By equally sharing domestic activities 'maternal thinking' also develops in fathers, and with that, he stressed, the meaning of gender similarly begins to change. In his later study he explored 'role-sharing' in dual-career families with school-aged children (Coltrane, 1990: 157-181). He analysed the division of labour with reference to couples' accounts of how and why they attempt to share child-care and housework. He found that postponing the transition to parenthood facilitated task-sharing, by encouraging men to become attached to the father role and by promoting women's efforts to relinquish full responsibilities for household management. He also reported that the practice of child-care increased fathers' sensitivity and attachment to the father role.

Hocschild discovered that the happiest two-job families were those in which men and women managed 'the second shift' through sharing and taking responsibility, and 'good communication' (Hocschild, 1989: 270). She discovered that there were some women and men who used a variety of strategies to get what they wanted out of marriage and family life. Women 'played helpless', became 'supermoms', 'cut back at paid work', and 'cut back at housework, marriage, self, and child, and sought paid and unpaid help.' Some men used strategies of co-operation and strategies of resistance such as disaffiliation, need reduction, substitute offering, and selective encouragement (Hocschild, 1989: 194-203). Negotiation of housework was not always without conflict and failure. When women failed to negotiate equal sharing of housework with their husbands, then believing in a 'family myth' and pretending that everything was 'fine' required an enormous amount of 'emotion work'-the work of *trying* (her emphasis) to feel the 'right' feeling. It is this 'emotion work'-that 'stands between the stalled revolution on the one hand, and broken marriages on the other' (Hocschild, 1989: 46).

What I am highlighting here is that finding solutions to household work contradictions requires much energy and hard work which can put strain on couples' already pressured lives. Bittman and Lovejoy (1991) interviewed 65 couples, asking if they discussed housework and child-care with one another; they also asked how they made decisions about 'who would do what' around the house. They found that a majority of respondents never discussed the allocation of chores. The respondents contended 'it just happens...sort of automatically'. One respondent confirmed that the domestic organisation in their household collapsed when she refused to do the unpaid housework (Bittman and Lovejoy, 1991). It appears that discussions and negotiation on household task allocation are areas where most couples choose to tread carefully.

Brennen and Moss (1991) studied the effect of dominant ideologies on women's experiences as mothers in full-time employment and the ways in which they interpreted that experience. They found contradictory ideologies within and between the private sphere and the public sphere that constrained as well as facilitated working mothers' abilities to combine paid work and unpaid work. They found that the 'organisation of time' and 'use of time' were the two strategies used to cope with the dual-earner lifestyle. Women used a number of strategies to organise their time. They went to bed earlier and got up earlier: cut down on their lunch hours; and brought work home. They also adopted methods to make the best use of time; lowered standards; cut out certain jobs; planned better to work more efficiently; used a routine; and worked more intensively. While some mothers were conscious of giving their children 'high quality' time, others reported that they 'wasted less time than they used to at work'. They found, overall, fathers were less likely to reduce or change their hours at work. Fathers assumed the role of assistant, helping out with some domestic work and child-care (Brennen and Moss, 1991: 184-191).

Mederer (1993: 136) suggests that when household labour allocation is considered as an independent variable it becomes part of the micro interaction in the family and implies connections with the macro structure of gender inequality. She found a significant relationship between housework allocation and perceptions of fairness. She reported 'the more housework women in her sample did, and the more time they spent doing it relative to their husbands, the more conflict they reported' (Mederer, 1993: 142). She confirmed that managing family life is an integral part of the female gender definitions (Mederer, 1993: 143). Negotiation of household division of labour is based on power, inequality and conflict, giving rise to contradictions that make matters worse for family members. One such contradiction between overtly stated values and privately maintained practices is a result of contemporary patriarchy that subordinates women within the framework of equality (Bittman and Lovejoy, 1993: 319).

Recently Goodnow and Bowes (1994) studied micro interactions of 50 housework-sharing couples to establish the dynamics of housework patterns. They analysed how couples felt about household jobs and the way they negotiated and rationalised sharing while dealing with structural constraints. They explored the ways couples departed from stereotypes by locating the motivating reasons for change, analysing styles of talk and negotiation, and understanding 'workface' factors such as availability, competence, and standards: factors that have been influencing both the shape of a work pattern and the points of tension that occur (Goodnow and Bowes, 1994: 5).

Furthermore they found that couples in their sample 'did not find one way and then stick with it forever. Nor did they expect that their current way would last forever' (Goodnow and Bowes 1994: 193). They mean that the couples negotiated tasks by following a few simple rules: Does this job need to be done? Who should get the job? How are we going to work it out between us? (Goodnow and Bowes, 1994: 72). They propose that the quality of relationship between partners 'is the thread that ties together references to the good relationship, to fairness, and to being treated as an individual with choice rather than as a type ('a woman', 'a man') to which certain jobs are attached' (Goodnow and Bowes, 1994: 122).

Studies from interactive approaches have made a significant contribution to the knowledge of the microprocesses that are at play in the negotiation and maintenance of gender divisions of labour in families. However, no study in its theoretical and methodological orientation comes close to resolving household work contradictions. Research reviewed in this chapter indicates a number of issues that explain a gender-based division of labour in families. It highlights why women choose to continue to take on household management responsibilities when they enter the labour force (Berheide, 1984; Hochschild, 1989).

It appears that household duties such as caring for other members are linked with women's identities as wives and mothers (Shaw, 1988: 333-337), and they therefore fear that conflict over housework maybe taken as not caring about their family (cf. Able and Nelson, 1990; Game and Pringle, 1983). This point is further developed by Mederer (1993) who sees that task performance and household management are two differing aspects of household labour. Her study shows that women reported unfairness on both task and management allocation, and conflict only on task allocation (Mederer, 1993: 133-145). This maybe because women have two identities, private nurturer and public self

(Mann, 1988: 286-317), and therefore breadwinning is not an integral part of women's role (Potuchek, 1992). Consequently employed women preserve their self concepts by accepting household management responsibilities without conflict and taking help from their significant others.

The need for an articulated approach

This book is informed by both Australian and overseas studies that have researched in the area of 'household work contradictions and its solutions'. But what this book intends to do is to link what we know about household work contradictions to the behind-the-scenes orchestration of solutions, in families in which both partners are involved in the labour market and responsible for family management. It takes a symbolic interactionist approach to interpreting life in three-job families, and connects it to the institutional (macro) order. This book also acknowledges studies that have taken into account both macro and micro aspects while explaining human behaviour (cf. Pestello and Voydanoff, 1991: 105-128). The concept of 'mesostructure' (Maines, 1982) is valuable for understanding how men and women merge their respective activities within the context of social constraints and create and enact a gendered division of labour. Further, it helps to understand how social structure is only understood through the process of its enactment by social participants (Maines, 1982: 276).

While using the symbolic interactionist framework, I will draw upon interactive studies and link the micro processes in the family to the macro social realities. At a methodological level this book uses in-depth open-ended interviewing techniques and a Grounded Theory (Glaser and Strauss, 1967) approach to analyse respondents' accounts. The focus will be to examine linkages and processes of articulation between the macro institutional order and the micro interaction order. This linkage will be used to graphically show how three-job families manage household work contradictions. This is an advance over the available conceptual frameworks in the study of families. In keeping with a Grounded Theory orientation a conceptual model will be developed in Chapter 3 that will articulate macro and micro domains to show how husbands and wives manage household work contradictions in three-job families.

20

3 Conceptual Framework and Central Claim

In Chapter 2, research into family dynamics was considered to find solutions to household work contradictions. This showed that families negotiate and use strategies in order to cope with household work contradictions. The contention of this chapter is that families, in the interaction order, devise effective household 'management rules' as strategies to solve household work contradictions. This claim has to be placed in the context of ongoing debates about the articulation of institutional and interaction orders. Therefore, I intend to develop a suitably broad framework which encompasses these two orders. To do this, I draw on some of the current theoretical debates on the relevant dualisms. I also incorporate insights from the interview transcripts as part of the process of developing a grounded theory.

After discussing the rationale, I select from the literature and synthesise the general framework in Figure 3.1. This is the context for my more specific claim (Figure 3.2) about the family rules and typological claim (Figure 3.3) about differences in household management styles of three-job families.

By characterising my claim in this conceptual framework I overcome the limits of the interaction order by linking it to the macro structures (institutional order). I do this by proposing a theoretical model (Figure 3.1) that describes the relationship of the macro institutional order and the micro interaction order as one of 'loose coupling'. The notion of loose-coupling between the macro institutional order and the micro interaction order as shown in Figure 3.1 is for analytical and clarity purposes. However, in practice, in families, this is to be seen as an absolute fusion. Figure 3.2 is about the specific claim regarding the particular situation of three-job families under study. In Figure 3.3, the theoretical and specific claim is extended, and two emergent models

(Trade-off and Rigid) are presented to demonstrate the differences between respondents' household management styles. In other words, Figures 3.1 through 3.3 provide a theoretical, specific and analytical argument to depict who manages household work contradictions in three-job families.

Rationale

I take an interactionist standpoint, developing an understanding of the interaction order that does justice to both the macro institutional order and the micro interaction order. I refer the actions of family members to some posited rules or precepts that enable them to 'go on' in social situations. I assume that three-job couples negotiate and make use of certain rules while achieving various goals with regard to managing household work contradictions. I use these rules to interpret their actions. Both the rules and the conceptual framework have been developed and clarified by continual immersion in the transcripts from the fieldwork.

Rules are written or unwritten laws or customs that guide or control behaviour or action. These rules can be found at the centre of Giddens's structuration theory (1979). Giddens perceives 'structure' as rules and resources that actors draw upon in their activities in order to produce and reproduce society. In other words, rules and resources enable people to do things, to make a difference in the social world (Layder, 1994: 139).

Rules and enablements pertain to both the macro institutional order and the micro interaction order. Institutional approaches conceptualise rules as rigid and prescribed guidelines, and claim that they are internalised by individuals through socialisation. Rules are also perceived by institutionalists as over-arching and superimposing on individuals' actions. In contrast, interactive approaches view rules as fluid, flexible and subject to continual negotiation and renegotiation. A difference between the two schools of thought leads us to the heart of an ongoing debate on 'dualism' in social theory.

22

Dualism in social theory

The concept of dualism is perceived in terms of two fundamental elements in existence in the world. In other words, it applies to any doctrine in which the fundamental forms of things, 'substances', 'reality', etc., are seen as of two contrasting types without any possibility of one being reduced to the other. A sociological dualism is concerned with the reality as seen from two perspectives: individual agency and the structural determination of social outcomes (Jary and Jary, 1991: 175). Long before the macro-micro debate began, the connection between levels of analysis represented a major interactionist concern. Strauss (1978) did not ignore the effects of structure on meanings and interactions and believed that macro-structures could be understood from a micro-analytic foundation. Also the founding of 'The Interaction Order' (Goffman, 1983) and the concept of 'interaction ritual chains' confronted the traditional concerns of sociology with social order, and argued that micro-interaction preceded structure (Collins, 1981). This was further referred to Blumer's (1969) emphasis on knitting together lines of action. Some interactionists have attempted to link macro-micro levels by postulating a middle level: the meso-structure (Maines, 1982), suggesting that a fixed distinction between the levels is misleading (Wiley, 1988).

In his discussion on dualisms in sociology, Layder suggests three oppositions: micro-macro, agency and structure, and individual-society. He contends that while micro analysis is concerned with the face to face encounters between people, a macro analysis concentrates on the larger and more general features of society like organisation, institutions and culture. Furthermore he suggests that the micro-macro dualism is related to the two other dualisms 'agency-structure' and 'individual-society' (Layder, 1994: 1-3).

Feminism's position on the macro-micro dualism

Socialist feminists focus on how the macro aspects of a society constrain women's options. However, in doing so, they tend to overlook the constraints and enablements of the micro interaction which are also at play. Those who have made theoretical links between public and private spheres have done so by connecting women's waged labour and

23

home life. Stacy (1981) and Beechey (1987) describe a structured accommodation between the labour market and domestic gender roles. Patriarchal ideology is seen to dominate in both spheres and to give rise to particular kinds of job structures in the labour market that tend to attract women and mothers as paid workers. Others see the workplace as a site of gender construction in which men's and women's identities are produced (Barrett and McIntosh, 1982). The interlinking of public and private spheres is a valuable concept in analysing tensions faced by women who combine paid and unpaid work. However, what remains to be done is to capture the actual processes of management of the conflicts and constraints that result from the contradictory nature of the two spheres that implicate both men and women.

Feminism's main aim of synthesising macro and micro orders is to give a picture of social organisation that combines economic activity with other forms of human social production (child-bearing, emotional sustenance, knowledge, household management, and sexuality and so on). It also perceives material production as linked with ideological production (Lengermann and Niebrugge-Brantley, 1992: 356). In other words, the tendency is to connect structure to interaction and consciousness.

Feminist sociologists' views of the macro-social order is one in which both social structure and ideology impact on individuals' perceptions of social reality. Its understanding of the micro-social order is markedly different from that of classical sociology (particularly symbolic interactionism). Being wives and mothers, women's experience of micro interaction is often responsive, intermittent, and based on inequality, because they inhabit separate worlds of meaning and experience constraint rather than choice in meaning-creating locations (Lengermann and Niebrugge-Brantley, 1992: 309-359).

Here, I discuss the work of Dorothy Smith on macro-micro connections. Her work is indicative of sociology's male-dominated nature as a profession and its exclusion of women in social theory. She claims that the 'problematic of the everyday world' (Smith, 1988) can only be understood in terms of the 'relations of ruling'. She focuses on the processes by which individuals' experiences are organised and influenced by the macro social structures as well as everyday practices. She suggests that in order to understand how the world is experienced by women it is necessary to 'explore how it is shaped in the extended relation of larger social and political relations' (Smith, 1988: 10).

24

Smith contends that macro-micro link should be understood from the direction of micro to macro and back to micro. This, she believes, is the way in which the local world of practices is implicated by the relations of ruling. She also argues that power is exercised at multiple sites, for example, 'a complex of organised practices, including government, law, business and financial organisation and educational institutions' as well as 'the discourses in texts that interpenetrate the multiple sites of power', (Smith, 1988: 3). She sees 'texts' providing the link between everyday experiences in a local setting and the organisation of rules that impact on individuals from the macro order of the society. I tend to agree with Smith's theorisation of the macro-micro connection, in that 'as subjects, as knowers, women are located in their everyday worlds rather than in an imaginary space constituted by the objectified forms of sociological knowledge built upon the relations of ruling apparatus and into its practices.'

Giddens's and the symbolic interactionists' position on the macro-micro dualism

In Giddens's structuration theory the idea of dualism poses a problem (1984: xx), as he argues against a distinction between agency and structure in favour of a duality which he calls the duality of structure. In this sense structure is intrinsically related to action and action is related to structure. Further, the analysis of social life is related to the interpretation of behaviour and the societal rules. From this it could be said that while sociology considers interpretative behaviour in explaining social life, it also takes into account the pre-existing nature of social institutions (Layder, 1994: 128).

Symbolic interactionism attempts to overcome the macro-micro dualism by perceiving individual and society as inseparable and indivisible (Cooley, 1902). Consequently the distinction between macro and micro processes is bogus, because by the usage of the term 'society', 'we are simply referring to the inter-linking of the social activities of many individuals' (Layder, 1994: 65). Symbolic interactionists developed the conception of society as held together by shared meanings. The concept of 'role-making' indicates the emergent behaviour of humans rather than their conforming to rigidly prescribed roles. As the emphasis is shifted from the simple process of enacting a prescribed role to creating it on the basis of attributed other-roles, the individual's own role definition never completely ceases (Turner, 1962: 21-23). This process depicts human action as being within a person's conscious control.

While contending with structuralism Blumer states his views on the image of human conduct as the follows:

> The linking of human group life to the operation of a mechanical structure, or the functioning of a system seeking equilibrium, seems to me to face grave difficulties in view of the formative and explorative character of interaction as the participants judge each other and guide their own acts by that judgement (Blumer, 1953: 199).

Symbolic interactionism considers structure as being modified through interaction, as well as providing the context for interaction to take place. The mutually interdependent relationship between society and individual requires that in order to understand either one, it is necessary to understand the other. Furthermore, the society is to be understood in terms of individuals comprising it, and individuals are to be understood as the members of a society (Meltzer, Petras, and Reynolds, 1975: 2). Thus, daily activities should be analysed as 'connected sequence over time and against the backcloth of various social settings' (Layder, 1993).

Structure provides the social context or conditions under which humans act. It incorporates large scale, more impersonal macro phenomena like social organisations, institutions and the distribution of power and resources, and cultural products. While the macro-micro distinction deals with a difference in level and scale of analysis and the research focus, the activity-structure distinction refers to both large-scale and small-scale features of social life (Layder, 1994: 5).

According to Giddens the term 'structure' is defined as follows:

> Structure. Rules and resources, recursively implicated in the reproduction of social systems. Structure exists only as memory traces, the organic basis of human knowledgeability, and as instantiated in action (Giddens, 1984: 377).

Giddens perceives structure as rules and resources that individuals use when they produce and reproduce society in their activities

(Giddens, 1984). He classified the resources which constitute structures of domination into two types: allocative and authoritative. He defined 'allocative' resources as those 'capabilities which generate command over objects or other material phenomena' (Giddens, 1979: 100). These are material objects (capital, raw material, land, assets) that give people the power to get things done. For example, ownership of means of production gives people the power to engage in enterprise. On the other hand, 'authoritative' resources refer to non-material factors (status, class, gender) that can give an individual a privileged or disadvantaged position in social organisation.

The concept of allocative resources is reformulated and simplified by Sewell as non-human resources such as objects, animate or inanimate, naturally occurring or manufactured, that can be used to enhance and maintain power (Sewell, 1992: 9). Sewell further develops Giddens's use of the term 'rules' as formally stated prescriptions in favour of 'informal not always conscious schemas, metaphors, or assumptions presupposed by such formal statements' (Sewell, 1992: 6). He distinguishes between 'cultural schemas' and 'resources', while treating both as a part of social structure (Sewell, 1992: 1-29). He perceives agents as empowered to act with and against others by structures, as they have the knowledge of schemas, which means the ability to apply them to new contexts. Although Sewell prefers the concept of 'schemas' instead of 'rules' it is somewhat similar to Giddens's notion of 'knowledgeability':

> Everything which actors know (believe) about the circumstances of their action and that of others, drawn upon in the production and reproduction of that action, including tacit as well as discursively available knowledge (Giddens, 1984: 375).

Sewell (1992: 21) also argues that the knowledge of cultural schemas implies the ability to act creatively. He commends the work of Goffman (1959, 1967) who demonstrated that all members of society employ complex repertoires of interactional skills to control and sustain ongoing relations (Sewell, 1992: 24).

Hays argues for a conception of structure as more than a pattern of material, objective, and external constraints engendering human passivity. She conceptualises the structure in three ways. First, structures are created by individuals and individuals are affected by

27

structures. In other words, people produce certain social structures while social structures produce certain types of individuals. Second, structures should be perceived as both facilitating as well as constraining. For example, although gender division gives people a status and a particular sense of identity it also constrains them to act in certain ways. Third, she takes Sewell's (1992) point to explain different levels of structures in that 'structures are more or less open to intentional and unintentional human tinkering' (Hays, 1994).

The relationship between the institutional and interaction orders can be perceived as similar to the structure-action dualism. Writers who have analysed social organisations (see Glaser and Strauss, 1967, 1968; Strauss, Schatzman, Ehrlich, Butcher and Sabshin, 1973; Becker, 1953) consider structure as something that is constantly 'in process'. For example, they consider a hospital social organisation as a 'structural process'. Hospital staff and patients are continually negotiating and bargaining with one another about the 'rules', meanings and circumstances that constrain their daily activities. In this case the institutional (hospital) order is continually being negotiated, and the hospital staff and patients are creating and recreating it in an ongoing manner. Similarly Thomas's (1984) study of maximum security prisons shows several negotiating styles.

'Negotiated order' is a useful concept in explaining how members of an organisation negotiate their own interpretation of social order. According to Strauss:

> The negotiated order on any given day could be conceived of as the sum total of the organisation's rules and policies, along with whatever agreements, understandings, pacts, contracts, and other working arrangements currently obtained (Strauss, 1978: 5-6).

Although the concept of 'negotiated order' has been used to explain the workings of total institutions (Strauss, 1978) it also indicates generally how social structure is generated and maintained. Furthermore, negotiated order is a useful tool in portraying how social orders emerge and become processed in the 'mesostructure' of organisational life (Thomas, 1984).

Mesostructure is that intermediate area in which the latency of negotiation arises in response to structural and interactional conditions without favouring structure or process (Maines, 1982). The concept of mesostructure demands that all structures decree through interaction and therefore represent the 'interpenetration of structure and process' (Maines, 1982). Pestello and Voydanoff argue that researchers incorporate into their analyses the diverse, pragmatic solutions that family members employ to economically survive and maintain a household, because families are shaped by the imposed patterning mechanisms of gender roles, division of labour and stratification provided by the society (Pestello and Voydanoff, 1991).

As a sociological theory symbolic interactionism is not without criticism. One example is that it overestimates the power of individuals to create their own realities and ignores the way in which meanings are influenced by structural inequalities of power and wealth (LaRossa and Reitzes, 1993: 154). It is also claimed that symbolic interactionism deals inadequately with power issues in that it does not postulate any connection between face-to-face interaction and structural features (Layder, 1994: 73). Layder stresses that it is because symbolic interactionism does not adequately deal with the macro-micro issue that it is taken to an anti-theoretical extreme (Layder, 1994: 74).

Erving Goffman considers the macro-micro worlds as distinct but of equal importance. Because Goffman was concerned with the nature and dynamics of interpersonal encounters, he portrayed the world as seen by the actors. Goffman believed in the fundamental importance of distinguishing between different kinds of social orders. However, he spent most of his time in the description and analysis of the interaction order (Layder, 1994: 181). He was concerned with social interaction, that is the social situation in which 'two or more individuals are physically in one another's response presence' (Goffman, 1983: 2). He perceived this as 'the interaction order' which is a substantive domain in its own right. He further contends that the interaction order has well-defined limits and inner workings and mechanisms which are not only derived from the domain itself but mould it as well.

According to Rawls there are four elements embedded in Goffman's conception of the interaction order. First, there are the social needs of the self. Second, there is the ability of the interaction order to be durable and to possess the capacity to resist external threats. Third, there are meanings that arise from the mutual interaction of participants. Fourth, it is concerned with the exploitative side of human nature (Rawls, 1987).

Layder (1994: 173-178) portrays the intersection of the interaction order and other social orders as the basis of a loose coupling with the macro institutional order. The concept of loose coupling implies a loose fit or spillage between structures and interaction, and it makes researchers aware of the consequence of the tensions between social structures (e.g., Thomas, 1984; Goldin and Thomas, 1984; Rubin, 1979).

In his discussion of the agency-structure dualism Layder (1994: 2-6) proposed two principal questions. First, how does human activity shape the very social circumstances in which it takes place? Second, how do the social circumstances in which activity takes place make certain things possible and rule out others? With regard to the connection of social structures (macro order) and interaction order (micro order) Goffman (1983: 11) claimed that social structures do not 'determine' culturally standard displays; they merely help people to select from an available repertoire of them.

Goffman distinguishes between two aspects of the macro institutional order that are external to the interaction order. These are general resources such as language and shared cultural knowledge that facilitates face to face interaction. This only takes place within the backdrop of wider 'extra-situational' resources that are cognitive and cultural in nature. The baggage of previous encounters is another source of extra-situational influence that affects the face to face interaction. These extra-situational resources are important features of the macro institutional order that are loosely coupled with the workings of the micro interaction order. I will now develop a conceptual framework for the purpose of this book.

Conceptual framework

To begin I take the humanist strand (Chicago School) rather than the approach of the Iowa School. Humanists reject any dualist position and construct a viable alternative, attending to the delicate interweaving between the institutional features of the society and the creative capacities of people far more than other structural approaches (Layder, 1994: 65). I believe that I have addressed symbolic interactionism's weaknesses by using a conceptual framework that recognises the importance of structural features such as viriarchy, patriarchy, gender divisions, power relations, resource constraints and job structure. I have also discussed feminism's position on macro-micro dualism and taken into account the very insightful work of Dorothy Smith in developing a conceptual framework for the study undertaken in this book. I particularly value the concept of 'relations of ruling' (Smith, 1988), which forms the backcloth of gender inequality inherent in the macro institutional order.

In this book macro structures are those patterned features of society (like viriarchy, patriarchy, gender relations, power relations, job structure, equal opportunity in the labour market) that facilitate or constrain the social actions of three-job couples. 'Viriarchy' is the masculine gender-system in which 'men control women by virtue of being husbands rather than by virtue of being fathers' (Waters, 1989: 211). Although the three-job family is conceived as a private realm it is also embedded in the larger social world. Keeping within symbolic interactionism I also regard three-job couples as being made up of active individuals creating and recreating the above mentioned features by continually negotiating and renegotiating social action with one another and other members of society. I work from the position of the micro interaction order and specify how three-job couples perceive and handle various structural constraints as they manage their households. In this book, the institutional order is seen as superimposing on the family interaction order, and members are seen as interpreting, negotiating and living within societal constraints. I shall invoke both the allocative resources (time, money, and energy) and authoritative resources (status or hierarchical position of family members) that pertain to the interaction order and affect the management of three-job households.

Although 'negotiated order' and 'mesostructures' are valuable concepts for studying macro-micro levels simultaneously, I favour Goffman's 'interaction order' approach to the study of three-job family life. Because the focus in this book is particularly on the 'interactive order' it allows me to perceive the family interaction order as a social realm that has its own constraints and enablements. Goffman's notion of loose coupling between the macro institutional order and the micro interaction order allows us to recognise that neither of the orders is free from the influence of the other, but rather that they depend on each other (Goffman, 1983). By taking this framework, I believe, I will be in a better position to portray three-job family life.

31

To begin, I discuss the general claim (Figure 3. 1). As this book is concerned with family members' face-to-face behaviour, I am working from the micro interaction order level upwards to the macro institutional order level and perceive the two levels as loosely coupled and of equal importance (Goffman, 1983).

Goffman (1983) views the interaction order as a domain in itself. Interaction order is comprised of perceived constraints, meanings, motivational forces: need for sense of identity and need to adjust, adapt, and cooperate (Turner, 1987: 15-27). There are other features such as self-other, role-relationships, rules and resources (Giddens, 1984), and ground rules and moral obligations that are also accounted for during interaction.

Goffman views two aspects that are external to the domain of face-to-face interaction also known as 'the interaction order' (D). The first aspect identifies the 'general' resources (A) that individuals in the interaction order (D) draw upon (via path f) as a means of managing encounters with others. This proceeds (via path e) from the backdrop of wider 'extra-situational' resources (B). Previous encounters (C) also known as the 'baggage of prior dealings' are another source (via path g) of extra-situational resources (B) that individuals draw upon (via path h) while managing their encounters in the interaction order (D). The nature and outcome/result (M) of the interaction order can be viewed (via path l) which feeds back (via path k) to impact on its overall operation.

The relationship between extra-situational resources (B) and the interaction order (D) is subject to loose coupling. This can be seen as individuals in interaction order (D) draw upon resources (via path j) and feedback (via path i) while 'making it happen'. This link is subject to filtering upwards and downwards between the orders giving rise to and arising from the conditions under which they both operate (Layder, 1994: 180). Goffman is clear that although the interaction order is a domain in itself it is never completely an independent order, because in some situations the influence of certain structural arrangements and other attributes which are of massive significance outside the situation will get through (Goffman, 1983: 14). Goffman perceives the link between interactional practices and structural patterns as 'a set of transformation rules, or a membrane' selecting how various externally relevant social distinctions will be managed within the interaction (Goffman, 1983: 11). The loosely coupled link is shown by the 'interfacing membrane' (n).

Giddens (1987) criticised Goffman's idea of an interaction order. He perceives the interaction order as only a partially independent domain in its own right because of its implications for the reproduction of institutional order. Although it is correct to say that Goffman does not draw out these implications, 'his framework is capable of dealing with system reproduction in the way that Giddens suggests' (Layder, 1994: 180). Also Goffman's stress on the loose coupling between the interaction order and the extra-situational resources and their mutual influence on each other does take into account the 'reproduction of structural or institutional order' (Goffman, 1983: 4-5).

Rawls (1987) agrees with Goffman in presuming that the interaction order is a domain in its own right, and in particular with the idea that the interaction order contains a different order of constraints (needs of social self for example) than that provided by the institutional order. Although these constraints, commitments and obligations differ in nature from the constraints of the institutional order, they are directly implicated in each other. It can be claimed that the two orders are merely interdependent because both tend to influence each other.

The distinctiveness of Goffman's work is in the notion of loose coupling that suggests that both the institutional order and the interaction order are distinct and yet interwoven aspects of society. The filtering upwards and downwards between the two orders allows for operating variations in accordance with empirical evidence (Layder, 1994: 180).

Specific claim

In extending the explanation (people make rules) to a specific claim, I wish to maintain the notion of loose coupling between the macro institutional order and the micro interaction order. In this case a loose coupling is shown between the society (institutional order) and the family (face-to-face interaction).

The essential features of Figure 3.2 illustrate the way in which family interaction order is connected to the institutional order. The family interaction order (D) is a domain in itself which comprises both household management rules and resources (authoritative and allocative) which form the operations of the family. It contains interactional constraints, commitments to family responsibilities and obligations, which may or may not be directly implicated by the institutional order. Above all, it also contains contradictions deriving from both the institutional order, and from the interactions themselves.

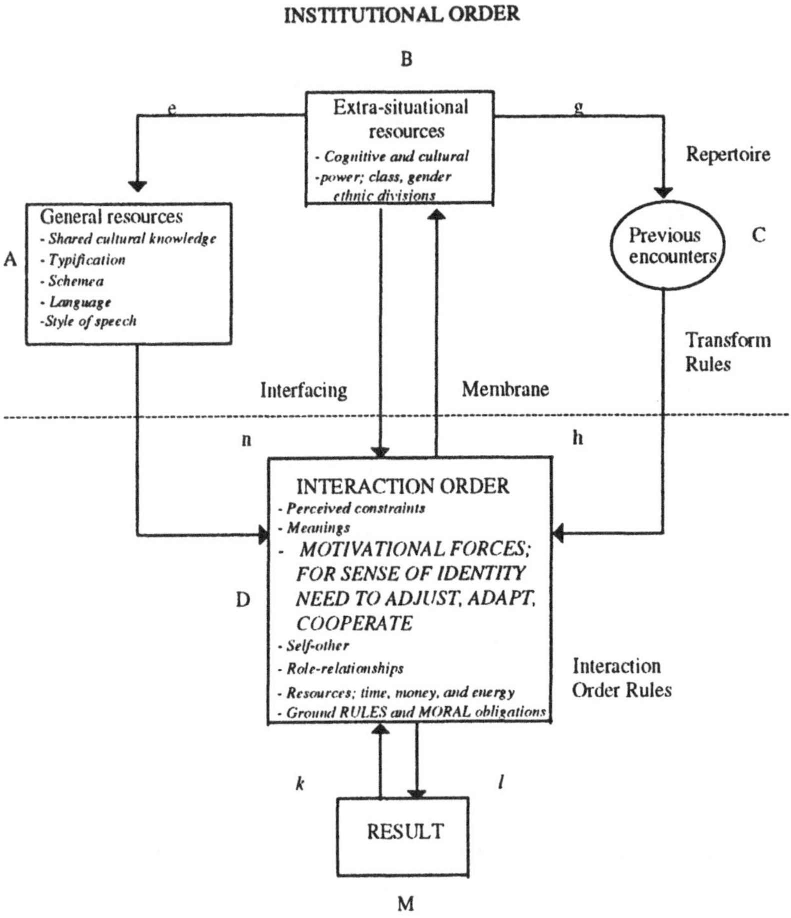

INSTITUTIONAL ORDER

B

e · · · · · Extra-situational resources · · · · · g

Repertoire

- *Cognitive and cultural*
- *power; class, gender*
  ethnic divisions

General resources
- *Shared cultural knowledge*
A - *Typification*
- *Schemea*
- *Language*
- *Style of speech*

Previous encounters C

Transform Rules

Interfacing   Membrane

n   h

INTERACTION ORDER
- *Perceived constraints*
- *Meanings*
- *MOTIVATIONAL FORCES;*
  FOR SENSE OF IDENTITY
D *NEED TO ADJUST, ADAPT,*
  COOPERATE
- *Self-other*
- *Role-relationships*   Interaction
- *Resources; time, money, and energy*   Order Rules
- *Ground RULES and MORAL obligations*

k   l

RESULT

M

Figure 3.1
LOOSE COUPLING BETWEEN THE
INSTITUTIONAL ORDER AND THE INTERACTION ORDER

A = General resources, B = Extra-situational resources,
C = Previous, D = Interaction order rules, M= Result

34

There are also the motivating forces: a need for sense of identity and a need to adjust, adapt, and cooperate which influence how individuals present themselves and interact with others (Turner, 1987: 15-27). Self-other refers to husband/wife and their partners. Being the main actors, partners' perceptions of self-roles and other-roles are vital in understanding the workings of the family interaction order. Similarly, the family role-relationships are important and need to be assessed to see if they are renegotiated or sustained. The allocative resources of time, money, and energy are the means by which three-job couples manage family interaction order. Similarly, status pertaining to gender and hierarchical position is an authoritative resource that influences the face-to-face interaction of family members.

Couples in family interaction order (D) draw upon (via path f) general resources (A) such as cultural traditions as ways of doing things. Cultural knowledge is the means by which husbands and wives manage encounters with one another. They also use typification to construct realities or to modify the existing patterns as marital partners and as parents. Individuals are supplied with specific sets of typifications and criteria of relevance, predefined by the society and made available to them for the ordering of the everyday life (Berger and Kellner, 1964: 1-24). The knowledge of schemas implies the ability to act creatively (Sewell, 1992: 21). In the case of families, couples are seen as equipped with the 'knowledge of schemas' necessary in negotiating rules and strategies in order to deal with household work contradictions.

This proceeds (via path e) from the backdrop of wider extra-situational resources (B). Partners in the family interaction order (D) also draw upon (via path h) previous encounters (C) with others to sustain or modify their family management rules and practices. Partners in the family interaction order (D) are influenced (via path j) by macro institutional patterns or the extra-situational resources (B) such as viriarchy, patriarchy, job structure, job description, traditional role ideology and gender relations.

Family interaction order is likely to influence (via path i) extra-situational resources (B), as members set a precedent for new ways of doing things through the renegotiation of roles and child-rearing practices in the light of available means. The outcome of the family interaction order (D) can be seen (via path l) in effective household management (M) which feeds back (via path k) into (D) to maintain or improve the existing nature of family interaction order. Having said that, I make the following claim specific to the families in the present study: Couples devise a particular type of family interaction order 'loosely coupled' with the institutional order in order to manage their three-job households.

INSTITUTIONAL ORDER

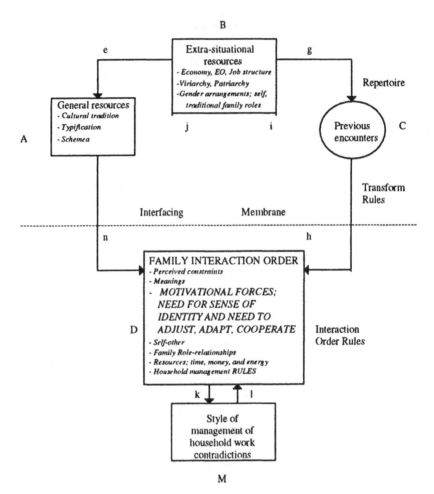

Figure 3.2
LOOSE COUPLING BETWEEN THE INSTITUTIONAL ORDER
AND THE FAMILY INTERACTION ORDER

A= General resources, B = Extra-situational resources, C = Previous encounters,
D = Interaction order rules, M = Effective management of household work contradictions

In the specific claim, I argue that all families worked out a particular kind of interaction order to manage their households. A particular kind of interaction order is mainly dependent on the type of household management rules the families work within. These rules are shaped by the institutional order and other components (constraints and enablements) of the family interaction order: motivation forces, self-other, family roles-relationships, and authoritative and allocative resources at hand.

Typological claim

In this section, I apply Figure 3.2 to the three-job families. I will compare two contrasting models (Trade-off and Rigid) of the family interaction order. The Trade-off Model leads to effective management and the Rigid Model leads to ineffective management of household work contradictions.

Figure 3.3 shows that the three-job families in the Trade-off Model have a set of rules that lead to effective management of household work contradictions. What is also evident from Figure 3.3 is the nature of household management rules. These rules are numbered 5 to 9 in order to key them with appropriate analysis chapters. Families in the Trade-off Model are judicious, realistic, and prepared to renegotiate roles and the ground rules. They have a shared sense of household problems and make use of flexible patterns as well as long-term strategies. In contrast, families in the Rigid Model try to achieve unlimited ends with limited means as they fail to successfully handle role overload and dilemmas, are unable to renegotiate roles and the ground rules, disagree on household problems and make use of rigid patterns and short term strategies only to manage their households ineffectively (P) via path q. Furthermore they fail to learn (via path o) from their inefficient behaviour (P). This is why I have characterised household rules negatively as unrealistic, inflexible etc. It can be claimed that 'the nature of household management rules makes a significant difference in the handling of the household work contradictions in three-job families'.

It is the argument of this book that both orders (macro and micro) affected one another. However, at times the influence of one was allowed to penetrate the other while at other times the influence was blocked. Furthermore three-job couples used prior experience, cultural knowledge, typification and schemas, allocative resources, and other interactive resources pertaining to both the macro institutional order and the micro interaction order as enablements to deal with internal and external constraints. In the rest of the book, I will use argument and evidence to support these claims, but I will first defend the methods used in the study.

INSTITUTIONAL ORDER

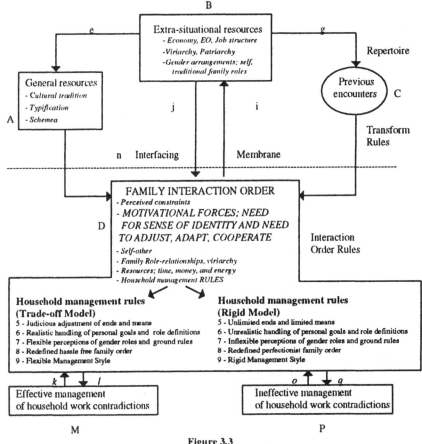

Figure 3.3
TYPOLOGY OF RULES IN
THE FAMILY INTERACTION ORDER

A = General resources, B = Extra-situational resources, C = Previous encounters
D = Interaction order rules, M = Effective management of household work contradictions,
P = Ineffective management of household work contradictions

38

4 Research Philosophy and Methodology

In this chapter, I am going to discuss research philosophy and methodology for the study on which this book is based. I will then discuss the problems of appropriate methods, including issues of validity and Grounded Theory. Then I will describe the relevant parts of the actual research process. I will conclude by describing the procedure by which the 'family models' and 'household management rules' emerged as a part of the theory building process.

Rationale

In this book, I use methods appropriate to the symbolic interactionist perspective to investigate who manages household work contradictions in three-job families. I do this by ascertaining the unspoken rules and meanings that emerge from the interactional accounts of three-job families.

What is the appropriate method?

Symbolic interactionist methods

Blumer emphasised the need for 'feeling one's way inside the experience of the actor' in order to see the world as the actor sees it (Blumer, 1969). Through some form of sympathetic introspection, the researcher must take the standpoint of the actor to capture that actor's world of meaning. Keeping in mind Blumer's insistence on sympathetic introspection, a researcher must use appropriate observational techniques such as life histories, autobiographies, case studies, diaries, letters, interviews and participant observation (Blumer, 1969: 26-26).

Validity of naturalistic investigation all-around

Although it is claimed that the problem of validity is not serious when referring to field observation (Hardyck and Petrinovich, 1975: 74-75), the problem of valid responses remains to be addressed. The validity of a measure depends upon the instrument used in studying a phenomena that is 'obviously' providing valid data (Kirk and Miller, 1990: 20). Measurement techniques exhibit theoretical validity if the theoretical paradigm is in correspondence with observations (Cronbach and Meehl, 1955).

It has been argued that using methods in combination provides a more full, all-around perspective on social phenomena while cross-validating each other around a common reference point (Finch and Mason, 1993; Kellaher, Peace, and Willcocks, 1990). However, combining different methods does not produce a more objective account; the account maybe more full but not necessarily more accurate (Fielding and Fielding, 1986).

The rationale for the methods used in the present study is based on the assumption that the structures of everyday meaning are held to represent reality and therefore the fieldwork, in part, was undertaken as 'a vehicle for entering the reality' (Rock, 1979: 184-194). I was interested in exploring the 'real' experiences and dynamics of three-job family way of life, and used qualitative methods such as some participant observation and intensive interviews. Furthermore, a questionnaire administered to assess the 'household division of labour' of three-job families was used as an aid to maximise validity. On receiving the filled questionnaires, I double checked any doubts regarding the performance of household tasks as I compared notes with respondents' accounts from transcriptions.

The connection with grounded theory

In this book, I have used methods in combination. In other words, I received three-job families' responses to the management of household work contradictions through intensive interviews, and cross validated them with household division of labour using a structured questionnaire.

Such validation may not have been feasible without using a combination of methods.

Grounded Theory is a scientific method when its procedures are carefully carried out. It is an approach by which empiricists maintain credibility. Finch and Mason (1990) used theoretical sampling as a strategy from Grounded Theory (Strauss and Corbin, 1990) to find 'negative cases' to refute or amend their interpretations. According to Habermas (1982: 269-70), validity claims are based on the sincerity and authenticity of a person's world of subjective experiences. I have used the Grounded Theory approach (Glaser and Strauss, 1967: 238-39) to analyse respondents' accounts and bring forth their sincere and authentic experiences of three-job family life.

The research process

The research problem was to explore the ways in which household work contradictions affected the everyday lives of three-job families, and who was responsible for managing these contradictions. During field-work I approached substantive and theoretical problems with a range of methods that are 'appropriate' for exploring three-job household management processes (Burgess, 1984: 143-165). The present study is based on the Grounded Theory model (Glaser and Strauss, 1967: 230), which is the discovery of theory from data, depicting the nature of structures that maybe discovered in everyday life. Grounded Theory is inductively derived from the study of the phenomenon it represents, and meets four central criteria: fit, understanding, generality, and control (see Glaser and Strauss, 1967: 236-250, and Glaser, 1978: 3). This approach is sympathetic to the theoretical framework used in the present study. To select sample families, I used a 'theoretical sampling' technique based on a Grounded Theory approach. According to Glaser and Strauss (1967: 45):

> Theoretical sampling is the process of data collection for generation of theory whereby the analyst jointly collects, codes and analyses his data and decides what data to collect next and where to find them, in order to develop his (sic) theory as it emerges.

This method is not only appropriate under certain field conditions but also preferable for specific purposes. It necessarily involves the selection of individuals or groups because they fit the categories, selected for their relevance in this case to providing understanding to the three-job family way of life.

Selection of families

Committing families that met the requirements of the present study posed some difficulties. The initial response from the couples was positive but, after realising their commitment and what it involved, some excused themselves due to a lack of time. Some couples deliberately did not wish to discuss their households because they feared the study might 'trigger' something. A certain degree of uneasiness was evident from both men and women as they responded reluctantly, e.g., 'Oh we are fine, thank you'.

The purpose of this research was generation of theory rather than the testing of existing theories, so the 'theoretical sampling' technique suggested by Glaser and Strauss (1967: 45) was used to select families. In order to have a manageable number of families, the range of variables was limited to include families in which heterosexual married couples: a) participated in the labour market either part-time or full-time, b) had dependent child/ren living with them at the time of the study, c) had been living together for at least two years, and d) were white Australians. These variables were kept constant if a 'snow-ball' effect took place while selecting families (Biernack and Waldorf, 1981). At the end, I had managed to interview 34 three-job couples.

Because three-job couples have limited time I felt asking them to spare an evening for an interview may have been unreasonable. For this reason it was appropriate to give them the choice of a convenient time and the flexibility for further variations. One incident helped me become more organised for further interviews. When I went to interview the Richards, Mrs. Richards informed me that her husband was held up at work and would not be back till very late. We agreed to meet the following week. As I came to their house for the second time she was surprised to see me as she had forgotten about the meeting. Luckily Mr. Richards came to the door and pressed for the interview, blaming his wife for not keeping things in order. He put it to his wife: 'This is the second time Gurjeet has come so we are not going to send her away; you can prepare for tomorrow's swimming class later.' In this way I had first hand experience of a three-job family handling an unexpected demand that took away most of their late evening. I also learned that these demands had a 'chain reaction' property, which had to be taken care of promptly in order to avoid further disorganisation.

After this, I telephoned respondents to confirm that they still wished to meet with me that evening. This gave them the liberty to say no if something had come up and/or to make another time. In this way the respondents were not under any pressure or obligation from my side. This sympathetic approach took great pressure off them. In fact this strategy proved to be quite a useful one.

Some families postponed and set another date for varying reasons such as: 'We are very unorganised today', 'We are having unexpected visitors and I am not sure how long they will stay', 'Could we make another day as I am very tired today', 'Our children are not well', 'My husband has flu' and so on. This process helped because by so doing we moved another step towards informality and a mutual understanding. Through such interactions I found that in three-job families only the women ran the daily routines and made household-related decisions. My similar personal situation of being a member of a three-job family helped a great deal, as the respondents felt I was one of them and therefore I understood things their way. They would often comment 'I am sure you can understand', 'We are all in the same boat', etc. This similarity with their 'situation' further promoted their support for the study. So after this 'getting in', or what Lofland and Lofland (1984: 20-29) called 'gaining the acceptance of people being studied', there was a comfortable interaction with respondents during later visits.

Table 4.1 gives an overview of the interviewees. More detail on the background characteristics of respondents is given in Tables 4.2-4.7.

Since current life stage was considered as an important factor in this study respondents from a wide range of age group were included. From Table 4.2 it can be observed that women's age varied from 26-49 whereas for men it was 29-51. Although a majority of the males in the sample were slightly older compared to the females in seven cases they were younger compared to their partners. This age variation was observed in couples who had remarried. With regard to the marital status of couples all 34 couples were married.

43

Table 4.1 Families Interviewed

Families	Husband's occupation	Hours/ week	Age	Wife's occupation	Hours/ week	Age	No. of children
Burton	Editor	37	38	Lecturer	40	32	1
Knight	Lecturer	50	37	Teacher	10+	36	3
Giles	Plumber	50	36	Admin. assistant	15+	32	2
Simmons	Lecturer	40+	37	Lecturer	40+	37	3
Stone	Policeman	40	44	Admin assistant	18	36	2
Broom	Lecturer	40+	38	Home-care worker	25	38	3
Faldo	Lecturer	40	46	Manager	40	44	2
Long	Business consultant	60	36	Lecturer	40	43	3
Jenning	Professor	40+	44	Teacher	10	34	3
Harris	Salesman	40+	42	Nurse	10+	36	1
Yeoman	Tutor	30	36	Home-care worker	15+	38	6
Fielding	Shed-hand	50+	30	Admin. assistant	30	26	3
Jeffery	Roof-tiler	30	47	Child-minder	36	41	3
Simpson	Salesman	54	40	Teacher	35	36	3
Jackson	Bookkeeper	20	33	Secretary	20	35	2
Donovan	Builder	50	38	Secretary	25	37	2
Stacy	Salesman	60	29	Sales woman	26	28	1
James	Gardner	50+	48	Lecturer	35+	36	2
Sands	Social worker	40	36	Nurse	38	32	1
Drummond	Salesman	38	40	Library assistant	20	33	1
Richards	Scientist	35	43	Teacher	35	40	2
Short	Sales assistant	25	42	Home-care worker	10	41	3
Mason	Foreman	50+	36	Nurse	35	35	2
Black	Lecturer	40+	34	Technician	10+	35	3
Ferguson	Salesman	38	38	Teacher	23	33	3
Kerrington	Scientist	60+	45	Technician	15+	49	3
Davidson	Teacher	38	48	Teacher	25	44	3
White	Professor	40+	44	Teacher	45	44	3
Fields	Lecturer	40+	45	Teacher	40	43	3
Hope	Carpenter	37	36	Lay-out designer	38	30	3
Turner	Salesman	43	29	Security officer	35	41	2
Turnbull	Technician	37+	30	Information officer	20	38	1
Brown	Teacher	35	37	Teacher	20	34	2
Wills	Businessman	40+	51	Business woman	45+	48	2

Table 4.2 Age of Husbands and Wives

	26-31	32-37	38-43	44-49	50-55
Husbands (N=34)	4	10	9	10	1
Wives (N=34)	3	16	9	6	0

Educational status of couples ranged from Year 8 to Ph.D qualifications (Table 4.3). More males compared to their partners had attained qualifications below secondary level whereas an equal number of males and females had received secondary school certificate. Tertiary qualifications were obtained by more females in the sample. The number of males in receiving postgraduate qualifications is almost double.

Table 4.3 Educational Status of Husbands and Wives

	Year 8	Secondary	Graduates	Post-Graduates
Husbands (N=34)	6	8	13	7
Wives (N=34)	2	8	20	4

On the four-class model of Australian society (Australian Bureau of Statistics, 1983) females scored higher than their partners did (see Table 4.3).

Table 4.4 Occupational Status of Husbands and Wives

	Bourgeois Managerial	Professional/ collar	White collar	Blue
Husbands (N=34)	0	13	12	9
Wives (N=34)	0	15	11	8

Table 4.5 shows that slightly less than half of the females, in the sample, worked up to 25 hours/week. On the other hand roughly half the males in the sample, had employment commitments of 36-46 hours/week. Overall male respondents were involved in paid work for more hours than women respondents.

Table 4.5 Employment (hours/week) of Husbands and Wives

	0-25	26-36	36-46	46-56	56+
Husbands (N=34)	0	3	15	9	7
Wives (N=34)	14	11	8	1	0

Table 4.6 shows a variation in the earnings of husbands and wives. As women were involved in part-time employment and tended to slowly increase their paid work hours their earnings/ week were lesser than those of their partners.

Table 4.6 Earnings ($/week) of Husbands and Wives

	less than 100	100-200	200-300	300-400	400+
Husbands (N=34)	0	0	4	8	22
Wives (N=34)	4	1	7	9	13

Table 4.7 shows that a majority of husbands and wives belonged to the religious denomination of Roman Catholic. One female and one male belonged to Baha'i. Approximately one third of respondents showed no religious affiliation.

Table 4.7 Religious Background of Husbands and Wives

	Roman Catholic	Anglican	Presbyterian	Others	None
Husbands (N-34)	17	2	1	1	13
Wives (N=34)	15	5	4	1	9

The sample families can be described as European, heterosexual, married, and employed couples with 2.3 children with an over-representation of Roman Catholics.

Research techniques

I used intensive interviews to elicit from the respondents rich and detailed material (Lofland and Lofland, 1984: 12) on the processes of management of household work contradictions in their families. I also used some participant observation as a pivotal strategy in the interactionist tradition (Rock, 1979: 178) to enter the emerging worlds of three-job families.

Furthermore, a structured questionnaire was used to assess members' household task performance, and the results were compared with their accounts from the interviews. The bulk of information was gathered through intensive interviewing, some participant observation, and formal and informal contacts with the respondents. The two modes of inquiry, 'exploration' and 'inspection', are the means to a genuinely rigorous sense of naturalistic examination of the empirical social world (Blumer, 1969: 40-47).

Exploration: participant observation

The main purpose of the exploratory study is to gain a clear understanding of the problem, of relevant data and of related concepts in the light of the knowledge acquired by the researcher (Blumer, 1969: 40). On acquiring the role of a participant observer the researcher's main concern is in rendering meaningful the world of the informant. This method as a sociological device chiefly associated with the programme of symbolic interactionism (Rock, 1979: 178-179) mirrors other pragmatist processes, because it turns to praxis and away from speculation. Participant observation involves some form of natural social interaction with those being studied. Indirect observation can only be obtained from perceptive persons called informants who are present at the scene in the absence of researcher (McCall and Simmons, 1969: 4). In the present study my role was that of an indirect observer.

During the visits and interview sessions I was vigilant capturing the respondents' 'definition of situation' and interaction with one another. My presence in respondents' homes further validated their responses as I interviewed them in their natural family setting. In this way, I actively sought out and made notes on interaction among family members and their physical environment. I also participated in the same community and personally shared experiences with respondents.

I came across different kinds of men and women who made up this community. I learned the flexible, fluid and adaptable nature of three-job families. I experienced with them the various strategies that they had employed in order to adjust to various problematic situations.

I also added to my journal any information that I received at the school gate, shopping centres, check outs at local stores, barbecues, or with my close friends and acquaintances. At the time of each contact, I explored the 'processes' of respondents becoming a three-job family. From the very nature of this ongoing process I learned that they tackled, negotiated and solved problematic situations in their own unique ways. This gave me the opportunity of understanding the reality of their personal and social worlds, resources, and the coping strategies that they used to manage their households. In fact once the 'ice was broken' the troubled mothers and bothered husbands opened up a 'Pandora's box'. I exploited this opportunity to 'lift the veils' (Blumer, 1969: 41) off their household management styles.

My role as an incomplete observer was legitimate as I had gained access to their private arenas with their consent as an intensive conversational interviewer. As I talked to them I observed their familial interaction, physical surroundings, conversations over the telephones, and their hospitality. During the time I was at their homes their daily routine continued, e.g., their children came and interacted with them, their neighbours 'dropped in', their pets needed feeding and their babies woke up. At such moments I made notes in order to capture the impact of the unexpected demand, to record their conjugal interaction, and to know how and by whom the problem was resolved. This gave me first hand experience of a three-job family life. In this way I 'grasped the setting' and understood their personal situation (Douglas, 1976: 123-124).

During the 'exploration' stage I contacted various child-care services to inquire about the child-care needs of families in the area. I learned that many families were on the waiting lists. The director of the University child-care centre disclosed that their waiting list had more than hundred names. I also learned that there was an acute shortage in the number of places held by the local child-care centres in the age group of birth to three.

I also chatted to the owners' local family restaurants, and learned that during their 'specials' more families came to eat out than ever before. This maybe an indication of families' desire to avoid unnecessary chores if given the opportunity to use cost-effective ways of feeding themselves. I also found that at the local school lunch orders are mostly from the children of employed parents. The local grocery stores had also extended their business hours to facilitate the 'rushed wife'. I kept records of the press reports, non-academic articles, women's magazines, television and radio programmes and talk-back shows relevant to employed parents. I made notes on information given to women on how to carry the 'double duty', beat the physical fatigue, stress and tensions, and above all ways to become a 'superwoman'. Often an occasional article would appear in women's magazines about the 'man in your life', and 'how to involve him in the household work without hassles'. The media treated such families as under pressure and vulnerable.

I also talked to the local stores about the kind of customers they received. They revealed that there were at least two kinds of women who come to their stores: one who came to buy and the other who came to pry, and those who do not buy are not employed. They also felt that they could identify an employed woman from her dress and from the fact that she would usually be in a rush. In order to get non-employed women's opinion towards employed women I often chatted to them and learned that they sometimes resented them for their material wealth. Through exploration, I shared respondents' everyday life experiences in the community. I became an acute observer and tried to gain a wider picture of three-job family way of life through discussions with members of the community which provided the answers to theoretical questions (Blumer, 1969: 41-42).

Inspection: intensive interviewing

Consistent with interactionism, the main research technique used to acquire data collection in the present study was intensive conversational interviewing (Denzin, 1989: 43). I interviewed the informants in their own homes where we creatively and openly discussed their family experiences in search of mutual understanding (Douglas, 1985: 15). Intensive interviewing tends to focus on the understanding of 'sympathetic introspection' and imaginative reconstruction of 'definition of the situation' to emphasise one of the basic underlying assumptions of human behaviour. In order to enhance validity, I followed Douglas's advice on the skills with which I conducted the conversational interviews. First, I was clear about the goal, design, sample, and methods of analysis of the study, and I personally and solely conducted the interview discussions. Second, I was a motivated interviewer and had personal interest in the study that kept my enthusiasm. Third, I believe, my previous experience in field-work helped me become an adequate interviewer. I undertook the interview discussions with a 'common-sense' approach which is the most effective technique in the 'informal discussions' (Douglas, 1973: 374-379).

The interviews were carried out over a span of six months between 1990-1991. An open-ended interview guide was used to interview couples to gather information on their three-job family life. Permission to use a tape recorder was sought from respondents (Lofland and Lofland, 1984: 58-60). Because a joint session is very revealing of familial processes (Piotrkowski, 1979: 298) husband and wife were interviewed together. In this way the micro processes of the negotiation of family roles and household management strategies were captured which would have been missed otherwise (Richards, 1985: 25-27). The interviews lasted from a minimum of one hour to a maximum of three hours. A structured questionnaire to assess families' household division of labour was left with the couples and collected later.

My ethnicity further enriched the data as the informants described more deeply and clearly the Australian way of life giving historical background to the contemporary family life style. I believe my age and status as employed mother and a wife with young children helped me come closer to the respondents as they treated me 'in the same boat': leading a similar way of life.

Being a woman researcher posed few problems as the topic was within the boundaries of my gender, unlike areas traditionally 'off limits' to women investigators (Morgan, 1981: 87-113). Being a woman and sharing similar experiences actually gave me access to the information which a man may not have obtained (Finch, 1984: 77). For further validation of their responses I met some women respondents over coffee, cooking sessions, or lunches and talked about general familial problems and joys. Conversational interviews were conducted over a cup of coffee which, in the majority of cases, was prepared by husbands. This created an informal atmosphere which helped to develop a shared understanding and strengthened my role as a researcher to the researched (Corbin, 1971; Oakley, 1981; Finch, 1984).

Recording and transcription

Through recording, I was able to attend to respondents during the conversational interview session as well take notes if required. I found recording very useful since I accumulated much information from the informal talk. The respondents did not show any concern about recording and understood its necessity. Sometimes during the interview sessions the children made comments on the questions put to their parents, and I included these if they were vital, relevant, and/or contradictory. In four cases children voluntarily mentioned their contribution to the household division of labour. Overall, impression from children's accounts further validated couples' responses and enriched the family life under scrutiny. When the conversational interview closed, the themes on that family's situation were summarised. These analytical memos became useful during transcription of interview tapes and actual analysis (Glaser and Strauss, 1967: 108). I then transcribed the audio tapes verbatim.

Analysis

The data were analysed by methods prescribed by Strauss and Corbin (1990: 195-260), Lofland and Lofland (1984: 129-138), and Glaser and Strauss (1967: 110-128), as well as interpretive interactionism (Denzin, 1989). The focus of analysis was on interpretation of lived experiences involving people in an ongoing symbolic interaction. In the initial stages of analysis, memos and diagrams took several forms, with regard to families' household management styles, coping strategies and categorisation of family models (Strauss and Corbin, 1990: 198).

Since the main emphasis of the present study was to capture three-job families' experiences of managing household work contradictions, it was necessary to treat the families as separate entities. Therefore the case study method was used to capture the entire phenomenon under investigation. It is this method which is a direct and all-around study of life-histories (Cooley, 1927: 316-317). This method is justified further by Angell, who argued that data on 'interactive behaviour' can only come from 'sympathetic insight' through using some form of the case method (Angell, 1936: 204). The 'constant comparison' method (Glaser and Strauss, 1967: 101-105) was used to interpret respondents' accounts, in order to detect emergent categories and typification as well as household management rules.

Given the large amount of transcribed material, I set out to discover the initial codes on 'what was happening' with regard to the management of household work contradictions in three-job families. I started by organising couples' responses under several questions: 'How did they manage their household and family responsibilities?' What constraints did they experience? How did they negotiate goals, identities and dilemmas? How did they allocate their resources? How did they decide on household division of labour? How did they negotiate the ground rules? What strategies did they use and what was the nature of these strategies? How did they manage to keep a normal atmosphere in the family? How did they define their three-job situation? What happened when the going got tough? What was the nature of their family and household experiences? How did they handle stress? Who took charge if/when life got to an unbearable stage? What was the description of a situation when coping with household work became difficult? Several other leading sub-enquires emerged from this process, which required further explanations into the management of three-job family life.

From the initial coding process, I discovered all families experienced varying degrees of problems in managing the household work contradictions. Their responses were categorised on the basis of five areas: what caused household work related problems; how often they experienced chaos; how bad it got; how they reacted; and what they did about it. I found that some families (20) experienced household work related problems infrequently and non-significantly (low intensity). I placed these families under Pattern One. The remaining families (14) experienced household work related problems quite often and, judging from their reactions, I learned that matters got worse (high intensity). I placed these families under Pattern Two.

I then turned to the data to see if some other factors had contributed to families' specific household situations. I found that all families experienced constraints, e.g., physical fatigue, stress, a lack of part-time job option especially for the wife, career demands, lack of adequate child-care, and money to buy adequate hired help in household work. On further inquiry, I found no correlation between respondents' occupation, education level, wives' paid work hours, family income, age or number of children and their particular household management style.

52

Table 4.8 Distribution of Trade-off and Rigid Rules According to Family Models

Family Model (No)	Family Name	Trade-off Rules					Rigid Rules			
		5	6	7	8	9	5	6	7	8
Trade-off (20)	Burton	+		+	+	+				
	Knight	+	+	+	+	+				
	Giles	+	+		+	+			+	
	Simmons	+	+	+	+	+				
	Stone	+	+		+	+			+	
	Broom	+	+	+	+	+				
	Faldo		+			+				
	Long		+	+						
	Jenning		+	+						
	Harris								+	
	Yeoman		+		+				+	
	Fielding							+		
	Jeffery		+		+		+			
	Simpson		+				+			
	Jackson	+		+		+			+	
	Donovan		+							
	Stacy	+		+			+			+
	James		+						+	
	Sands			+						
	Drummond		+							
Rigid (14)	Richard		+			+				
	Short					+	+	+	+	+
	Mason		+				+		+	+
	Black			+		+				+
	Ferguson						+		+	+
	Kerrington							+	+	
	Davidson							+	+	+
	White						+	+	+	+
	Fields						+	+	+	+
	Hope						+	+	+	+
	Turner						+		+	+
	Turnbull	+	+			+	+		+	+
	Brown		+	+				+	+	+
	Wills			+			+	+	+	+

I then focused on the household management rules of families. This process showed that families in Pattern One used a specific set of household management rules, and families in Pattern Two used a different set of household management rules. I also found that families in these two patterns used household management rules that were gradient (from flexible and negotiable to rigid and non-negotiable) in nature. Families in Pattern One and Pattern Two also showed a progression from being somewhat egalitarian, realistic, compromising and harmonious, to being traditional, unrealistic, uncompromising and chaotic in the ways in which they managed household work contradictions. I also discovered that families in Pattern One used a trade-off approach to negotiating their household management rules. On the other hand, families in Pattern Two worked within a rigid framework to negotiate their household management rules. In this way two models (Trade-off and Rigid) of household management rules emerged. This is evident from the household management rules (5-9, Figure 3.3) employed by families. The nature and progression of household management rules can be seen in Table 4.8. These rules are in agreement with respondents' accounts in Chapters 5-9.

The outcome of the nature of household management rules used by families can be seen from Ineffective/Effective management of household work contradictions in Figure 3.3. For the sake of simplicity and clarity, from here onwards, I refer families in Pattern One using Trade-off Rules as 'Trade-off families' and families in Pattern Two using Rigid Rules as 'Rigid families'.

The two models of household management rules (5-9, Trade-off and Rigid) used by families (Figure 3.3, family interaction order) will now be used to provide evidence of effective and ineffective styles of management of household work contradictions in the context of presentation in Chapters 5-9. The numbering of household management rules 5-9 is to match them with Chapters 5-9 in this book.

5 How Do Families Handle External and Internal Constraints?

In Chapter 3, I claimed that 'the nature of household management rules makes a significant difference in the handling of household work contradictions in three-job families'. In this chapter, I begin to provide evidence and argument for this claim by specifying the constraints experienced by husbands and wives in managing their three-job households. A 'constraint' is perceived as a restraint that stems from either or both macro institutional order/labour market and micro interaction order/family and impinges on the normal workings of three-job families. Beechey (1987) describes these constraints as structural tensions between the labour process, occupational and industrial concentrations of women employees and the sexual division of labour. These constraints affect a family's means and prevent the accomplishment of ends. Conceptually it can be claimed that members in the interaction order (D) in Figure 3.3 (Chapter 3) faced constraints at two levels. On the one hand they had to deal with constraints emerging at micro level, such as commitment to family obligations, the needs of self and a lack of allocative resources. At another level they had to handle constraints pertaining to the institutional order, such as viriarchy, patriarchy, gender ideology, job structure, lack of adequate on-site child-care facilities, and traditional family role ideology.

When linked across and within the macro and the micro orders, these constraints lead to household work contradictions. In order to deal with those contradictions the families have to handle these constraints. With reference to Figure 3.3, in Chapter 3, this chapter specifies how three-job families actually evaluate and deal with these constraints. This is where their assessment of the problem of managing household work contradictions begins.   I have three aims in this chapter: 1) to specify husbands' and wives' definitions of prime concerns and goals regarding work and family life; 2) to specify the means or a lack of means at hand in meeting these concerns and goals; and 3) to investigate those particular constraints that impede the means and hinder the accomplishment of husbands' and wives' personal goals.

These objectives will develop around the ways in which similar constraints impact on different families: how family-oriented wives (with traditional priorities) differ from self-motivated wives (with negotiable priorities) in perceiving and reacting to external and internal constraints. The emphasis will also be on how husbands' orientations to work and family roles (traditional or negotiable priorities) affect their feelings towards their wives' employment and achievement of goals. An overview of constraints experienced by families and their ends and means are presented in Table 5.1.

Table 5.1 Perceived Constraints/(Means) and Ends

Family Model (No.)	Family Name	Perceived Constraints/(Means)	Perceived Ends
Trade-off (20)	Burton	-Lack of proper child-care, only car, no bus service, financial worries, (parents help with child care)	-To have part-time work or more flexibility for both, career, for more time with children
	Giles	-(Hired help)	-Enjoy the fruits of labour
	Knight	-(Role sharing)	-Successful careers
	Faldo	-Lack of time -(Good relationships and communication)	-Maintain careers
	Stone	-(Part-time work)	-Economic independence -More family time for him
	Broom	-Inflexibility at work, a lack of regular part-time job for her, (husband shares housework and child-care, baby sitting club)	-A regular job for her
	Simmons	-(Equal sharing), school demands	-Successful careers
	Long	-Housework, no hired help, chore-list, husband's help	-Carer, family life, renovate the house, get through life

56

			stage with teenagers
	Jenning	-(Husband helps, work as a team) -No child-care	-Get through the early child bearing stage, gain full-time employment, re-establish family order
	Donovan	-Less time and energy, husband cannot cook, monotonous routine and no personal time	-Economic independence, and spend time with children
	Feilding	-(Husband and mother help), financial worries, small house	-Help husband supplement family income, get a bigger house
	Simpson	-Less time and a lack of job, meet dead lines, baby-sitter problems	-Personal time, more flexibility for him
	Harris	-Young baby	-go back to work full-time slowly and painlessly
	James	-Mortgage, child-care problems, lack of job flexibility for him	-Family time, personal time
Rigid (14)	Richards	-Less time and energy, insufficient hired help	-Leisure, time for kids' sports, be organised, and maintained order
	Short	-Only car, no hired help, husband studying, she works overtime, no money, young children	-Husband's study, personal and family time
	Mason	-Less time, young children	-Children's sports, home beautiful
	Black	-Young children, less time, money, and energy, no family support	-Pay off mortgage, job security, spend time with children
	Ferguson	-Have to work for money, less money and hefty mortgage	
	Kerrington	-Generation gap	-Children's welfare
	Davidson	-Lack of regular full-time job for her, lack of recognition of her paid work	-Get a regular full-time job to support children's education, self development
	White	-Very little time and energy, insufficient hired help	-Finish family routine on time and start music classes, beautiful home and garden, increase leisure, nutritious meal
	Fields	-Less time and energy, young	-Proper meals, kids' home

	children	work, study, clean home, garden, make money, give kids a good home life
Hope	-(Dishwasher and limited help from husband and children), lack of social network, young children	-Material things, children's needs, keep husband happy
Turner	-Tiredness, less physical strength, less time	-Maintain economic independence, make marriage work
Turnbull	-Less time and energy, young baby, financial pressures	-Economic independence, make marriage work
Brown	-No time during the week -Can't afford hired help, immobile because breast-feeding, meet dead lines, no family support	-Effective performance at work, time with kids, pay mortgage - Get through the week days
Willis	-Tiredness, insufficient hired help	-Maintain good business and the household

It was observed that families in Pattern One rearranged their priorities, worked within flexible roles, kept work and family life separate, learned from their limitations and were beginning to adjust to a three-job family life style. These families are to be perceived as close to the Trade-off Model, specifically rule one in Figure 3.3. In contrast, families in Pattern Two wished to achieve careers, good family life in the traditional sense, and a beautiful home. However, they worked within rigid and traditional roles and failed to learn from chaotic situations. These families are to be perceived close to the Rigid Model, specifically rule one in Figure 3.3.

Trade-off families

Trade-off families faced similar constraints as Rigid families did. However, these families continually assessed their priorities in the light of their means. For example, if they felt they were unable to cope with higher household work standards because they did not have sufficient resources, then they renegotiated and compromised with lower standards. Similarly, if they felt they ought to be spending more time with children then they cut down on their own social life. These families continually tried to maintain a balance between their means and ends.

'Part-time job is better'   The Burtons wished for either two part-time jobs or to have more flexibility at their paid work places so that they could spend more time with their two-year old daughter. At the time they felt a lack of control over their lives.

> Mrs. Burton: I would like my job to be part-time...or have more flexibility in hours. Part-time job is better when you have young children. So that when she (daughter) is this age I can start at eight and finish at four and Don (husband) can start at ten and finish at six so that she is in care from only ten to four.
> Mr. Burton: The other thing for us is to work part-time three days a week.

When Mrs. Burton started this job her options were either to be employed full-time or not at all. Even though a part-time situation would give them more time with their daughter it would not satisfy her career needs. They discussed problems related to part-time employment in terms of professional recognition. Mrs. Burton said: 'Often part-time workers are excluded, being lesser and not being given the sense of belonging.' They faced financial constraints in that they could not afford a second car. They also found the town bus service inadequate as the time-table did not suit them. If they could have used the bus to and from paid work then one partner would have the freedom of using the car for the entire day. They considered dropping and picking up each other a waste of time that they would rather spend with their daughter. In order to minimise their daughter's extended hours with the baby sitter they relied on Mrs. Burton's mother for two half days and one whole day a week.

Similarly, Mrs. Stone was employed part-time so that she could be home when the children returned from school. Having been employed nine-to-five for a few weeks recently Mrs. Stone felt it limited her family life. She preferred to be employed part-time so that the family could have a normal life. Her main goal was to be with her children, and keep her hand in the labour market for the time-being. By being employed part-time she was financially independent with her children.

Mr. Stone was employed to work on shifts and found it clashed with his duties in the family. He desired to spend more time with his two boys.

Mr. Stone: I think if I had the regular hours then I will be able to see the kids more often...you get to spend less time as I work shifts...sometimes I am going and they come home from school...or are getting up...or if I am going out when they are coming from school.

Mrs. Stone: It is not so bad because you have ordinary weeks as well.

They had deliberately renegotiated one and half jobs for Mrs. Stone so that they could pass through the 'young family' life stage as smoothly as possible. Once their children were self sufficient they would be able to help with household work and make life less hectic.

Mr. and Mrs. Broom had three small children. Mrs. Broom worked in the evenings as a home carer for the senior citizens. She wished for a more challenging type of employment that involved mind activity rather than physical labour. She said: 'It is not a job, I'd like something a little bit more mentally stimulating.' Her paid work involved helping incapacitated people care for themselves and their households. The only rewards she got from this job were to get away from the household for a few hours.

Mrs. Broom: I am lucky because Ken (husband) works at the university and he is pretty flexible. I send her (daughter) part-time...even that's very expensive. If I had to put her there full-time I don't think I could afford it.

She decided to wait for a few more years before starting full-time employment, till her youngest child went to school, so that she had more time on her hands.

'You got to have a goal in life' Mr. and Mrs. Giles had had their share of hardships and pressures in the past three years. However, through perseverance and co-operation they had managed to be where they wanted to be: succeeding in a plumbing business. Their present comfortable financial situation allowed them to hire someone to do their household work and gardening. They believed in the work ethic and felt one could achieve anything in life if they put their mind and hard work to it. Mr. Giles said: 'I think you enjoy fruits of labour but not if they are given to you.' A basic philosophy of 'the more you put into it the more you are going to get out of it', had turned their lives around.

Mrs. Giles: To be here now the way I am and what I have is what we have always planned. So everything that I have chosen to do has been in mind and this is where I wanted to be. Danny's (husband) family are very different, they haven't made any decisions.

Mr. Giles: You got to have a goal in your life.

Having gone through the process of becoming a successful business couple they had encountered endless problems, but by paying others to do their household work they were fairly happy with their present situation. The main constraint they faced now was a lack of time to enjoy the 'fruits of labour.'

Nature of household work

'There are no great rewards in doing the repetitive housework' The Simmons were a professional couple who had a somewhat different lifestyle compared to the other respondents. They shared household work and child-care almost equally. They had reduced the pressures through modifying their expectations, as well as by simplifying the household work.

Mr. Simmons: There are no great rewards in doing repetitive housework.

Mrs. Simmons: No, cleaning of the house is not rewarding...not rewarding at all.

Mr. Simmons: Not when you have young children.

Mrs. Simmons: Yes...I mean if you have something clean it will last five minutes...laughs...there is no point in having something shining if it is not going to last.

By sharing and cutting down the household work to an absolute minimum they concentrated on their paid work and obtained satisfaction from their careers. They also believed if they had free time they would rather spend it on doing 'enjoyable' activities such as gardening, rather than monotonous chores as household work. Considering the fact that they had three young children to care for as well as their careers they wished to be employed slightly less then full-time. However, this was not possible because as scientists they often had to stay back late. Mr. Simmons felt it is very demanding for people to be in full-time employment when they have young children. They complained that their children's school was always making demands for them to contribute as parents. Mrs. Simmons expected teachers to be more sympathetic to

61

parents' time: 'I think they don't give any consideration that both parents might be working.' By cutting down on tasks other than the essential the Simmons managed three children and two careers rather judiciously.

Mr. and Mrs. Faldo had two teenage children who were fairly independent and did not make many demands on their parents. Mrs. Faldo considered herself fortunate to be able to get a full-time position in a teaching profession. A lack of time was their only problem. They felt they spent a large chunk of their time doing the household work. One way in which they could save time was to hire someone to do the household work, but they knew they did not have spare cash to employ a full-time housekeeper. With children nearly off their hands they knew they were getting back to the freedom of 'childless years'.

Some families faced financial problems which may have affected their coping styles. Other constraints such as lack of child-care, small children, and job inflexibility were experienced by almost every family in the sample.

Mr. and Mrs. Long was employed full-time and had three children. Their main concerns at the time of this research were their careers and children. They believed household work was a burden that they tried to share through a chore list. Mrs. Long said: 'I think housework is something that needs to be done and I don't enjoy doing it and I don't find a great deal of satisfaction.' They talked about an ideal situation of leaving the housework to hired hands so that they could spend more time as a family. At the time of interview they felt they were very tired and stressed because in addition to their jobs they had been renovating their house.

The main constraint they experienced was the 'life stage' constraint. Their three teenage children demanded time and energy to be driven to various places, and while this was essential it was time consuming. They were waiting for the time when they would be through with this stage of life and children would be off their hands.

Mr. Long: There are a lot of things that we had deferred. We keep a close track as to how much time we have left until children are gone.
Mrs. Long: We only have eight years left...it is a long commitment. It gets less and less as kids gets older.
Mr. Long: And it is coming to an end we hope.

Once their children left home they would get back to their own way of life which they had postponed.

Mr. and Mrs. Donovan had been in the work force for many years before having their two children. Mr. Donovan felt disenchanted with the contemporary life style, as he compared his own situation with that of his parents' generation and believed their lives were now much more stressful.

> Mr. Donovan: There are enormous sort of financial pressures and it has become a consumer orientated society and you are basically materialist. The things that I didn't have as a child my children take for granted. So a lot of our motivations are financial.

Being the main provider he felt his role was limited to fulfilling the material needs of his family. He worked at a construction site six days a week and spent three nights at the technical college. He wished for an extra day in the week to really enjoy life.

Mrs. Donovan was solely responsible for home making and often had to rush to take care of a number of things in a short time. She never had the time to sit and relax or engage in recreational activities alone or with other members of her family. She found herself forever fulfilling her duties within a limited time. She said: 'Having more leisure time I think will make it a lot easier and it will be good for the family to have that time.' She also wished to break the monotony of everyday routine whereby she could make demands on others for a change.

> Mrs. Donovan: Often at work I'd say I am really bored of cooking every night. I think if you knew the meal you had prepared everyone would enjoy it would be different...but mind you the repetitions every night...and from my side I tend to fight this repetition.

She felt if her husband could learn to cook then she would have a break from the everyday routine. She had also enjoyed cooking the family meal, whereas now she found it was a chore that had to be done.

The Sands and the Drummonds had fewer household work problems because they had only one child each. Mrs. Drummond was employed part-time and was solely responsible for household management. She felt that her home-maker role restricted her in a number of ways. One was the nature of household work which she found to be very distressing. It was because of the short-lived nature of 'tidiness' and 'cleanliness' that led to her lack of control over her household environment. She also believed her husband pressured her to be a 'good wife' and a 'good home-maker'. She wanted to employ a full-time housekeeper so that she could do other things in her life besides being a wife and a mother. However, this was not possible because of the cost of employing someone to do their household work was beyond their current financial capacities.

Lack of adequate child-care

'It will work if there are a few more child-care centres' Mrs. Jenning was employed part-time because of her young children. However, at the time of this research she believed if she did not get full-time employment soon she never would. She believed that as women get older and out of touch with the professional world their chances of finding employment are reduced significantly. The main constraint she experienced was a lack of proper child-care service. She felt it was time the society recognised women's contribution to their families.

> Mrs. Jenning: I think women are going back to two-incomes and it will work if there are few more child-care centres. It would be a social recognition of family responsibilities that women have.

At the time of interview she was on a long waiting list for a place in the day-care centre. Similarly, Mrs. Harris was waiting for a place in a family day-care centre, she had been asked to wait up to ten months to get her son a place in the centre. Having given up her high-paying job to start a family Mrs. Harris had become dependent on her husband. Her new role as a mother confined her to the house with a baby.

> Mrs. Harris: Being at home you sort of miss the adult company. The children can be very demanding. Maybe because Mark (son) is our first baby or what? And I have to continually have an eye on him.

In the meantime finding the right child minder was her biggest problem. Although she had her name on the waiting list at the local family day-care service she was unsure when or if she would get a place for her son. Presently she had to rely on a private person with whom she was not very happy because she had too many children under her care.

Mr. and Mrs. Simpson were in full-time employment and had three children. Mr. Simpson worked as a manager at the local petrol station which required his attendance till late afternoons. He was under stress because of the pressure to keep up with the tyranny of the clock.

> Mr. Simpson: There should be a situation where you don't have to meet dead lines and hours and things like that...you know well...if I don't turn up at work at 7.30 am the roof is not going to cave-in. And if I want to go somewhere and knock off at four o' clock instead of half past six...I should be able to do so. I mean if I have that flexibility which I don't have now.

A lack of time was their main constraint. They wished for an extra few hours a day so that Mr. Simpson could spend more time with the family. He also wished he could cook so that he could take some pressure off his wife. They often had to stay up late for the next day's preparations and therefore did not sit down to relax. Mrs. Simpson said: 'We need more hours in the day to catch up on sleep.' Another constraint was that their baby-sitter was leaving town. Mrs. Simpson said: 'Our baby sitter is about to disappear which is a real shame because we will have the problem of looking for another one. As it is, there is a real shortage of child-care centres.' They also wished for more free time so that they could do things together both as a family and as individuals.

Similarly, Mr and Mrs. James worked full-time and faced after-school and holiday child-care problems. They believed if they had relatives or close family members then they could rely on them in case of emergencies. They also wished for a child-care service where children could be left while recovering from minor ailments. Leaving sick children with friends or sending them to school was inappropriate. They faced a unique problem of home repairs as they are at paid work from nine to five.

> Mrs. James: When you are at work you can't have people over to fix things for you. You have to be at home when a plumber or a builder comes. It is very hard and you have to stay home from work...and if they are late you are stuck and you never know when they are going to turn up.

Mr. James earned only a moderate income and therefore they needed a second income to pay off the mortgage. Their house also required maintenance and yet they could not find free time to be home when a person could come and do the necessary repairs.

Child-care responsibilities

'Looking after children is not an easy job'   Mrs. Fielding joined the labour force in order to supplement the family income. She would have to pay a large sum of money to someone to mind her three children. To avoid this she had to rely on her husband to stay with the children while she went out to work. Mr. Fielding, a farm hand, could spare the time but lacked confidence in caring for small children and felt frustrated. However, it had made him realise mothering was not an easy job.

> Mr. Fielding: In the last few weeks I had stayed home all day and found it really hard to manage on my own. I now appreciate what Monica (wife) does. Looking after children is not an easy job.

Mr. Fielding believed he was not 'cut out' to be a carer and a nurturer as he was never around to experience or share child-rearing with his wife. He felt he was the outdoor type who escaped most of the time whenever there was a conflict with the children. Having to stay home and take over family responsibilities limited his wishes to be the provider in the family.

Economic constraints also affected their ability to buy a bigger house. They were living in a small three bedroom house which was not big enough for their three growing children. At the time of this research they were going through a difficult period because of the drought that had left Mr. Fielding without being employed for days. However, they held on to their hopes and believed that once the draught was over and children were at school they could get back to two incomes and be able to afford a bigger place.

Rigid families

Families in this pattern wished to achieve many goals with somewhat limited ends. The specific constraints were a lack of resources: time, energy, and money to buy hired help. While some families often negotiated household work and renegotiated priorities because of limited means, others struggled to achieve too many goals with limited resources.

'You have to be highly organised'   Mr. and Mrs. Richards were a career-oriented couple with two children. They were both in full time employment. Over the years they had developed a particular set of rules regarding their own family order. This system had become a way of life without which they would be in disarray. However it constrained their lives in two ways. First, it was a constant pressure to abide by these rules. Second, because of the rigid routine that they felt compelled to follow there was a lack of time and energy for other activities such as leisure. These two constraints were interdependent, in that they both resulted from leading a mechanical life style. Mrs. Richards said: 'You have to be highly organised and I tend to be more regimented and I like the sense of order, but I feel tired.'

During week days they rushed around doing their usual tasks plus the next day's preparation. They often found themselves relying on takeaway meals and hired help in order to remain highly organised. The takeaway factor added to their stress as they believed it was an indicator of their inefficiency. They often discussed with one another the restrictions household work had placed on their time together as a couple and as a family. Sometimes Mrs. Richards felt guilty for not being able to perform regular chores which they found themselves often catching up with at the weekend.

> Mrs. Richards: Leisure is one thing we don't often have time for. Andrew (husband) likes to work outdoors or in the garage on the weekends. He is busy doing his things and I am tidying up inside. Basically we don't have the time...the children go and play with their friends and we sometimes sit and watch TV but there is no time really.
> Mr. Richards: We encourage the children for organised sports and we would take them and pick them up but we don't get involved.

Being caught up in the need to maintain a high level of organisation they were not motivated to do or enjoy other things. However, they had some peace of mind, even if it was under a regimented schedule.

Similarly, the Masons had to be extremely organised to get through the day. Most of their time revolved around children and their sporting

67

activities. They felt they had to consider their children and their needs rather than have their own leisure. They recalled childless years when they did not have children as they could take off to various places. Now that they were in employment and raising two small children they found time a very scarce resource. Mrs. Mason believed children's homework should be done on time so that they did not suffer academically. Organisation of various events needed time and energy which was always scarce. Mrs. Mason said: 'There is a pressure of thinking ahead at all times knowing that you are going to be busy and you have to make sure you got your baby sitter so that the pressure is taken off you.' She believed in order to survive as a three-job family they needed to be alert at all times.

Mr. and Mrs. Short had three children under the age of 10. With their two small incomes they managed to keep themselves afloat, but could not afford a second car. They had to organise so that they could both have an access to their only car. Sometimes their schedules clashed as Mr. Short needed the car to go to the university and at the same time his wife had to be somewhere else. Mrs. Short felt she could not even express her feelings because she believed her husband had the right to the car.

She worked evening shifts so that her husband could be with the children. This meant Mr. Short was unable to concentrate on his academic work while minding the children.

> Mr. Short: If I can get more organised and get my work done...that would make a big difference...that's the whole issue.

He felt guilty for not spending quality time on his academic work. On the other hand they did not have the money to pay a baby sitter.. He believed that once he earned enough money his wife wouldn't need to be employed and he would take care of his family like a man.

Having to work in a dead-end job, a lack of a second car, her husband's attitude towards household work, and a lack of personal and family time made Mrs. Short feel trapped. This feeling of frustration was in conflict with her goal of helping her husband upgrade his qualifications. However, she saw they did not have any choice but to manage like this for another few years.

Mr. and Mrs. Black were raising three children and found themselves hard pressed for time, money and energy. Mr. Black was a research scientist who often had to work overtime and therefore could not help his wife with the household work regularly. Their main priority was raising their three children under eight. Mrs. Black had to take them with her every where she went, e.g., shopping or going down the street to fetch something. Although Mrs. Black was employed only part-time she found it extremely difficult to keep up with everything.

By the time they completed the daily routine they had no time or energy left to be motivated to do anything else. Mr. Black said: 'Organising a vegetable area is something that just can't be done because there is no time.' Mrs. Black wished they had enough money so that they could employ someone to help them out: 'If I had someone to do the ironing...I think I should be able to have a few luxuries.' Having a few luxuries was perceived as sitting and having a cup of coffee or finishing a drink without forgetting it. They also wished to have their parents or relatives in the same town so that they could call upon them in emergencies, especially when they had had enough of everything.

Mr. and Mrs. Ferguson were mainly employed for economic necessity. Although they had a reasonable family income, with three children and a high mortgage they barely managed. Mr. Ferguson felt that his insufficient income constrained his wife's choice to stay home and do other things.

Mr. Ferguson: Things would be easier if we win a lotto...to own our home. If people didn't have to buy their homes then life would be easier.

Mrs. Ferguson: If I didn't have to work for money then I would still work but I wouldn't have the pressure that I have to work.

Mrs. Ferguson felt the government should adequately reward families in similar situations who have young children. More tax rebates would give women the choice to be employed part-time or to stay home with children. They felt that due to economic constraints and the need to be employed they were not able to spend more time with their children to give them a good foundation in their earlier years. Mr. Ferguson said: 'I think if the family plays together it stays together.' Playing together meant spending time together as a unit that they saw as essential for the family to develop a good communication system.

Mrs. Ferguson: You got to have the time...especially when they come rushing in from school and they say this is what happened in the class

69

today. By the time you come home they have buried it in their mind or forgotten about it or it maybe too late.

Mr. Ferguson: Once you have got a bond like the baby and mother then they can spread out and they know that they can come back.

They believed that if they did not have the financial constraints they would be able to give their children more time because then Mrs. Ferguson would not have to be in the labour force till the children were a bit older. Then they would have quality time as a family.

Mrs. Brown felt she was carrying a high level of stress at all times, with too many demands and less time and energy to meet them. She found she was very efficient at her paid work and could meet the deadlines, but by the time she came home she was drained. She felt she was going through a stage when a number of demands, especially household routine and child-care tasks, exhausted her. Consequently she doubted her ability as a mother to carry out her duties properly and efficiently. She also had to be close to the baby for breast feeding.

Mrs. Brown: You have to accept that there are differences in men and women. Men don't have babies...the maternal thing...and because the female has these maternal instincts...their prime thing...the women have to accept it.

Accepting biological capabilities meant accepting the restrictions associated with breastfeeding. Although Mr. and Mrs. Brown earned two good incomes their financial situation was somewhat insecure. Approaching their forties the Browns believed they were rather old for starting a family and buying a house. Having led a life of luxury in their earlier years they felt trapped with financial difficulties and children's demands.

Mr. Brown: I think the financial stress is worse. If we had our mortgage paid, and basically I wish we had done all this when we were 22, or if we can wish for having relatives where you can dump the kids.

Mrs. Brown: If my father came and paid our mortgage it will be nice. I think for us it is hard because we are a little bit older when we started, we didn't have any money and borrowed all the money. We need some time to get out by ourselves.

They did not have a close social network where they could leave the

70

children and have some time on their own. They felt they would have been financially better off if Mrs. Brown had continued to work full-time and Mr. Brown had cut down his paid work hours to half-time in order to care for the children. Although their present means did not allow much choice they felt by having a couple of children they were a 'normal' family.

Lack of permanent employment for women

'Taking one day at a time'   The Kerringtons had three children of which two were teenagers. Their main concern was the children's welfare during their teenage years. They felt contemporary values restricted the individual's overall development. Mr. Kerrington believed that people were going through another dark age which was like a straight jacket. He felt people's thoughts are concentrated on the material world and their own selfish ends, and therefore had become very ego-centric and lacked world vision. He believed and dreaded the fact that his children were heading for disaster.

> Mr. Kerrington: A teenager will learn to risk and that will complicate things further. They can't always be stable because their hormones are setting them off and they tend to change all the time. They want to experience so much life in a short period of time and that causes conflict because we want to be over-protective.

Mrs. Kerrington feared that if they gave them too much freedom they might not appreciate the value of independence. They found it difficult to be consistent in terms of discipline. Mrs. Kerrington believed in gentle discipline whereas her husband found himself enforcing things on their children. Mrs. Kerrington was employed on a casual basis which involved uncertainty, irregularity and a lack of permanency. She enjoyed going out to work because she kept in touch with the outside world. However, with her job uncertainty she could not make long-term plans, and had to take 'one day at a time'. Casual employment was not only uncertain but also lower paid. It did not give her the benefits or the satisfaction of a regular job.

Mrs. Davidson had quit her job during child-bearing. However, she found getting back to the system (paid work) was extremely difficult. As a result of an interruption in her career she missed out on training

71

and experience. She found herself struggling to get permanent employment.

> Mrs. Davidson: I just want a little bit of security in employment because now I am only paid hourly rate and I spend a lot of time in the preparation which I am not paid for.

By being employed part-time she encountered the problem of presenting herself as an employed mother. She said: 'I would spend all afternoon at home for the preparations but because I am at home people think oh mum is at home so she can do the washing up and that sort of thing so it is a problem that I am home.' More importantly their financial situation needed a boost because two of their teenagers would be going to university. They planned to support their children through tertiary education.

Traditional gender ideology and a lack of resources contributed to some families' ineffective management of their three-job households. In addition to their employment and family commitments, the wives had involved themselves in other activities such as giving music lessons, improving qualifications, helping in husband's business, maintaining a hobby farm and so on. To make matters worse, they also wished to be within the traditional framework of being good wives and mothers, and home-makers. This posed problems because the time, money and energy did not permit them to run their households like the non-employed women could.

Hardships of three-job families

'A full-time housekeeper would be nice' Mr. and Mrs. White were a professional couple who had been in the paid work force for more than eighteen years. In addition to her job as a teacher Mrs. White took music lessons at her home in the evenings. Because she finished paid work at three pm her daily routine involved dropping and picking up children from various training venues after-school. In the hustle and bustle of shuttling children she did the daily shopping, planned, prepared and cooked the evening meal, fed everyone, and cleaned up before she commenced the music classes in the evening in her own home. She found there was not enough time to do all this before her pupils arrived for a lesson. On the other hand Mr. White, a university

professor, had to stay back at paid work many days a week to catch up with paper-work. He was therefore unable to come home on time and help his wife get organised.

> Mrs. White: Probably we go in circles sometimes...like if I finish teaching at say six thirty and I maybe having a bunch of kids at seven thirty for a concert and it is pretty hard to get the meal on the table, eat, get the dishes done, straighten up the place to look decent.

Even though she was able to get her children to help her if and when she needed, she found it difficult to keep things from overlapping. A certain rush to get things done had become a norm that led to a number of other problems. Mrs. White tried to keep her family life separate from her music lessons but found it extremely difficult. The problem was exacerbated because she converted a part of her family home into a public place to hold music classes. She tried to finish the family routine before the lesson began but felt physically tired and mentally drained. Although Mr. White could come home on time some days, he did not take on major household responsibilities. He confessed that at times he was pressured to come home at three pm which disrupted his paid work priorities. Mr. White said he probably would like to go to his office and catch up on his paper-work when he got the time over the weekend.

They were aware of a lack of resources and tried to relieve some of the household work pressure by hiring someone to do it. Although this was of some assistance it was not enough to ease the pressure off. Mrs. White said: 'We really need a full-time house keeper', but this was beyond their financial capacity. They also wanted a beautiful garden and more leisure but had to consider this beyond their present life style.

Mrs. White felt that household work was a major hindrance for the accomplishment of her main interest of tutoring classical music to children. She also wished to present her home as tidy as possible to her pupils and their parents. This desire exacerbated household work problems. Her own music interests and the needs of her family clashed, because on the one hand she wanted to provide her husband and children with a good home life and nutritious home-cooked meals and on the other hand she wished to present herself as an excellent music teacher who lived in a beautiful home. The problem was that her husband had a different set of priorities and did not share her ideas. Feeling strained, she sometimes pressured her husband and children to see things from her point of view. They enjoyed the rewards of music classes such as money, prestige, and a desirable life style, however these came at the cost of a lack of family time and energy on the part of Mrs. White.

Similarly, the Fields were a professional couple with three children. Whereas it was Mrs. White's music that caused problems in the Whites' household, it was Mrs. Fields' study commitments that added to their burden. Over the years as they became absorbed in their careers and their children grew older, their demands increased and ultimately time and energy became a scarce resource. Even when Mrs. Fields was employed full-time she managed to give her children the best of home life. As the children went to high school their extra-curricular activities increased. A lack of time was exacerbated by her own need to gain further qualifications for the next round of promotions. The demands of her family and children were increasingly becoming difficult to fulfil. Her desire to give the children a comfortable life required time and energy which was always consumed before she got around to doing things for them. As a result of a lack of time and physical energy she often experienced stress and anxiety. The need to catch up with the chores left in the morning rush, meal preparation, straightening of the household, next day's preparations, etc., got in the way when she wanted to just sit and relax and talk to the children about their day and their homework. She felt if they had a full-time housekeeper she could do the things she enjoyed most. Her wishes were to organise her life around teaching, making money and enjoying children. She felt household chores were a burden on all working mothers.

> Mrs. Fields: I think the absolute ideal thing is going to work and looking after children and not doing any housework. We tried to have hired help but then we decided we didn't want to spend that much money.

Household work was perceived undesirable but essential in order to give children a normal childhood. However, maintaining a higher living standard had become burdensome because it was a challenge that was beyond their means. She also desired a beautiful garden which was beyond her physical capabilities. Her lack of physical strength did not allow her to dig and shovel. This bothered her a great deal. Unwillingly, Mr. Fields would help her maintain the garden because he knew how much it meant to her. However, this became a source of conflict when

74

he could not do it because of a lack of time. He felt he should not spend hours in the garden when he was already spending enough time helping his wife with the household work and child-care. His career as a university professor demanded more time than he allocated at present. They knew they were going through a life stage when they had less time, money and energy. Soon their children would be off their hands and then Mrs. Fields would need paid work to keep herself busy. They believed their present constraints were transient and could be justified in exchange for long-term rewards.

The Hope household operated within a strict traditional framework. Mr. Hope was not in favour of his wife working to earn an income because he firmly believed this was only his responsibility. However, it was only because of her additional income that they moved up the social ladder. Mrs. Hope earned more than her husband, but suppressed her provider identity because it demeaned her husband's image. By asserting his identity as 'the boss' in their family Mr. Hope subscribed to the view that husband should fulfil the provider role. He perceived his wife's earning capacity oppressive to his own identity so he often down played her economic contribution.

To keep peace, Mrs. Hope announced that it was her responsibility to maintain the household and therefore she often made sure things were done properly. It was very important to her to give a stable and loving home life to their two children so that they could look back with pride. By being employed full-time she had limited time and energy to meet her household work standards. When she arrived home at five in the afternoon she found she was unable to fulfil the everyday routine without her husband's and children's help. Although they had pulled themselves out of the financial difficulties they were not yet well-off enough to pay someone to get the household work done. They also lacked a close social network to be able to ask friends and family to care for their children in case of an emergency. This pressured Mr. Hope because he had to rush from his place of paid work to pick up the children after-school. However, they considered this problem temporary because once their children were a little older they would be able to walk home by themselves.

'Life is not a bed of roses' The Turners had two children in their late teens about whom they did not have to worry. Their household also operated within the traditional framework. Being in her mid-life and

being employed full-time, Mrs. Turner had very little time and energy left to keep the household running smoothly and effectively. Having experienced a disastrous first marriage where she was financially dependent, she was determined to earn her own income. She believed she was capable of performing a number of chores around the house but by the time she got around to doing them she was exhausted: 'At the end of the day I feel totally drained to do anything else.' Also she felt incapacitated because she was unable to do some of the strength-requiring tasks such as wood chopping and lawn mowing. She felt handicapped in having to rely on her husband for help.

The Turnbulls were going through a stage when they faced too many demands with limited resources. They considered time was an important asset. After they finished their paid work in the late afternoon they were left with very little spare time for the usual family routine. They had a young son who needed constant attention from one of them. They felt they ought to give him personal attention and quality time to make up for his time spent with the baby sitter. However, with their tight schedule during the evenings they could spend time neither with their son nor with one another.

Mrs. Turnbull found household work boring and quite often she would neglect the every day cleaning which accumulated to a major chore. She lacked interest and enthusiasm in doing the household work and was quite happy to employ somebody else to do the whole lot. However, their current financial situation did not allow them this luxury. She enjoyed cooking but it led to other tasks such as 'having to clean up'. It also annoyed her when her husband constantly asked her the whereabouts of various things around the house. She felt her husband should be able to do more around the house because she was now being in the labour force.

> Mrs. Turnbull: Some of us still have to know where the butter is in the fridge...time and time you are opening the fridge and saying where is the butter...bend down and look... .

Things would have been different for them if their financial situation was better. In order to supplement their income they had a hobby farm that required much of their week ends. They both had to be employed to survive because even with their two incomes there was not enough money to employ a housekeeper in order to relieve them of the

76

household work burden. Mrs. Turnbull believed that no one had a 'life on a bed of roses'. Optimistically she said: 'Because it will be better in the long run that's why we are doing what we are doing and because that's life.' She knew that once her husband had finished his higher degree and their son had gone to school they would be back on their feet again.

'Anything for a quiet life'   Mr. and Mrs. Wills had a family business around which their lives revolved. In some ways they felt they should have started the business when they were younger and more resilient. Mr. Wills believed having a successful business woman for a wife was a personal constraint. He believed being a man it was his role to provide for his family. However, as it turned out the business initiated by his wife was their main source of income. Over the last few years as a business woman his wife had earned a respectable status in the community. In his bitterness he blamed women's independence to be the cause of men's downfall.

> Mr. Wills: I give in, anything for a quiet life. Those days are gone when we used to drive them to the fields and work all day and then they come home and cook a meal...and now they say clean this, do this, do that.

His wife's success in business was something that he never anticipated and therefore felt powerless. He believed his wife dominated in making decisions about family matters. He felt he was fighting a losing battle. He revealed that recently a decision to send their daughter overseas was not a democratic one because he had no say in it. On the other hand his wife believed it was a family business and therefore he should be pleased.

Conclusions

All families faced constraints resulting from both macro institutional and micro interaction orders. Constraints such as the needs of self, role-relationship, and resources pertaining to the micro interaction order were somewhat kept under control especially by Trade-off families. On the other hand constraints resulting from structures beyond their control such as job inflexibility, lack of child-care places, job structure pertaining to the macro institutional order were not easily managed. It can be said that Trade-off families were more realistic and that they constantly monitored their ends and means to manage their households effectively.

Lack of time and energy, money to pay for a housekeeper as well as children's demands were the main constraints faced by all families. The problem of a lack of child-care places was faced by couples raising young children. This was intensified by their need to find an 'ideal' baby sitter. A lack of close network of extended family and relatives made things even more difficult for couples who were employed full-time and had very young children.

A sharp contrast can be observed in the perceptions of Trade-off and Rigid families with regard to their prime concerns and goals. Trade-off families (Table 5.1), had realised their limitations much earlier and had made adjustments accordingly. They lowered household work standards and down-played the need to perform monotonous chores in order to increase and allocate means in essential areas. Rigid families (Table 5.1), wished to achieve a lot, without compromising and making necessary adjustments. They continued to struggle to achieve their targets at the cost of their own and family's well being. They had become accustomed to dealing with constraints frantically and finding solutions under pressure. This aspect will be further developed in Chapter 9.

Rigid families faced more problems in managing their households because of a number of constraints limiting their means. Husbands and wives in this pattern operated within a traditional division of labour and had a different set of priorities from each other. While the wives' inclination was both career and family, the husbands were mainly concerned about their own paid work. By taking on the double duty of paid and unpaid work the wives raised their husbands' and children's expectations. In addition, their desire to be good wives and mothers made it difficult for them to realise their personal goals.

Trade-off families appeared to be dealing with constraints successfully because they had reorganised their life style in a way that minimised the problems still faced by Rigid families. The wives had deliberately renegotiated their prime concerns to reduce additional responsibilities. In this way they extended the available means to deal with only the vital family issues. To some extent husbands and wives shared household work responsibilities and worked jointly. These families learned from their own and others' experiences of household work problems. Consequently they continually renegotiated their ends and evaluated their means. Rigid families, on the other hand, struggled to achieve many goals beyond their current means. This aspect will be elaborated in Chapter 7.

6 How Do Women Handle Personal Goals, Role Definitions and Dilemmas?

The women in my sample faced a varying degree of role-overload and dilemmas depending upon their involvement in the labour market, their life stage demands and their allocative resources (time, energy, money to buy adequate hired help). 'Role overload' simply means having more demands on one's time and energy than one can manage (Hood, 1983: 130). This chapter is about wives' dilemmas that resulted from a clash between their involvement in the labour force and commitment to family responsibilities. In order to resolve these dilemmas the wives had to deal with their personal goals and role definitions. With reference to rule 6 in Figure 3.3 in Chapter 3, this chapter specifies the ways in which wives dealt with their personal goals and role definitions.

There are three objectives of this chapter: 1) to investigate wives' current situation, personal goals, and their definitions of their role as wives and mothers, as well as the source (Table 6.1); 2) to investigate how attached or detached wives were to their paid work and family roles; and 3) to describe husbands' paid work and family priorities and their willingness to adjust to their wives' absence in the family. This chapter will also specify how wives experienced dilemmas, and what sources (such as socialisation) affected the ways in which they tried to manage their personal goals and role definitions. The differences in wives' handling of their personal goals and role definitions can be observed in Figure 3.3. By following rule 6, the wives in Trade-off families managed their personal goals and role definitions realistically. In contrast, wives in Rigid families handled their personal goals and role definitions unrealistically.

From Table 6.1 we can observe that all wives in the sample had somewhat similar personal goals with the exception of some wives (in Trade-off families) who referred to a joint goal (we) with their partners. While wives from Trade-off families related to fewer role commitments, the wives from Rigid families depict their attachment to a number of roles. Similarly, wives' source of knowledge ('mother's way of doing things') in Trade-off families was insignificant, positive and subtle, whereas wives' source of knowledge in Rigid families conflicted somewhat with their own perceptions of 'how things should be done'.

Table 6.1 Personal Goals, Role Definitions and Source of Knowledge

Family Model (No)	Family Name	Personal Goals	Role definitions	Source of knowledge
Trade-off (20)	Burton	-We came to this town with my job (W) -I will be bored at home (W) -I can't be home with my daughter (W)	-Mother, carer (W)	-I had a happy childhood (W)
	Giles	-We run a business (W) -I help him with the business (W)	-Family, help husband with business (W)	-My mum always baked cakes and biscuits for us (W)
	Simmons	-I am a career person (W)	-Successful career, family and home (W)	
	Broom	-I am earning my own income and it gives me a bit of confidence (W)	-Work, family (W)	-We lived in a communal home (W)
	Stone	-I work part-time to be with kids (W) -I work and raise children (W)	-Children, work (W)	
	Faldo	-I needed to go back to work for personal fulfilment and sanity (W)		
	Long	-I knew I will work (W) -I am no longer limited (W)	-Career, children, home (W)	

	Jenning	-I consider family peace and harmony highly so I work part-time (W) -I think women who work seek challenges beyond motherhood and children (W)	-Mother, home, work (W)	
	Fielding	-I wouldn't like to be the breadwinner (W)	-Good mother (W)	-My mother is a perfect mother (W)
	Simpson	-I knew I would be going back to work after kids (W)	-Relaxed home atmosphere for kids (W)	
	Donovan	-I work for economic reasons (W)		
	Drummond	-I work to get a break from the household (W)	-Home security, and family (W)	-My mother was a very warm person (W)
	Harris	-I enjoy going back to work even though the child care is a bit of a problem (W) -It is nice to see people other than your baby (W)	-Motherhood, son, work (W)	
	James	-I don't think it is nice to be begging money from the husband (W)		
Rigid (14)	Richards	-I knew I would go back to work after children (W)	-Work, children and clean home (W)	-Her mother always did voluntary work (H)
	Short	-I am helping with family income while he is studying (W) -It has added quality in me and my confidence has increased (W)	-Help husband study, work and family (W)	-I don't want to be like mum. Our house was clean but there wasn't love (W)
	Black	-I like to work to keep my mind active (W)	-Children and work (W)	
	Mason	-I would like to think I have my own money for things like a hair cut (W) -I wouldn't like to be dependent (W)	-Work, family, children and their sport (W)	-My mother was very strict (W)

82

Ferguson	-I have to work for money (W) -I enjoy the work but I want husband to earn the income (W)	-Mother, home and child care (W)	-His parents always shared the housework (W)
Kerrington	-I work to meet other people (W) -I work part-time to be with children (W)	-Mother, home and child care (W)	-My mother did not work to look after us (W)
Davidson	-I went back to work for economic independence and interest (W) -I work for kids' education (W)	-Mother, work (W)	-My family was very traditional (W)
White	-I work to make money (W) -I had something to do for myself (W)	-Home, work, music, family (W)	-Mother's cooking is more nutritious and balanced (W)
Fields	-I love working (W) -I had a secure job when I did (W)	-Work, study, family, home, garden (W)	-It is the way we are brought up (W)
Hope	-I needed to get away (W) -I felt inadequate at home (W)	-Home, children, husband happy (W)	-I was brought up with morals (W)
Turner	-I want to be financially independent (W)	-Home and peaceful marriage (W)	
Turnbull	-I was frustrated and quietly going round the twist (W) -I had to work for sanity (W)	-Caring for son and work (W)	-Mum wouldn't approve me asking husband for help (W)
Brown	-I knew I would go back after kids (W) -I want the kids to know that their mother is earning (W)	-Children, home, establish identity as a working mother (W)	-His mum doesn't approve of my earning capacity (W)
Wills	-I think women who are dependent on their husbands are far more subservient (W) -I think the business has helped me spiritually (W)	-Maintain economic independence (W)	

From wives' accounts in Table 6.1 it can then be suggested that it was both the source of knowledge and the objectives that intensified their dilemmas. In other words, the wives in Trade-off families were realistic about their personal goals and role demands. They related positively to the ways they had been brought up. They seemed to be managing their dilemmas effectively. In contrast, the wives in Rigid families were unrealistic about their personal goals and role demands. They tended to take on much more than what they possibly could do. They also tried to do 'everything' perfectly and tended to suffer the 'superwoman' syndrome.

Trade-off families

Wives under this model continually assessed their priorities in relation to their coping abilities and resources. If they were career-oriented they minimised their other roles so that they could manage paid work and family responsibilities effectively. Those who had young children preferred to be employed part-time so that they could spend more time with their children. They considered this essential mainly because of a lack of adequate and satisfactory child-care.

Employed mothers' guilt

'I hadn't had any baked cookies for the kids' Mrs. Burton, Mrs. Giles and Mrs. Drummond tried to create the same environment for their children in which they themselves had been brought up.

Mrs. Burton was in full-time employment. She compared her parenting standards with those of her mother. She was still coming to terms with the anguish and rewards she received by being an employed mother.

> Mrs. Burton: Sometimes women don't know how to cope with that change because you have a sense of being a modern mother. Personally, I have had a happy childhood and I think it is connected with the way my mother brought me up. But I am in a situation when I am employed and in conflict with that because I can't be at home with the children.

Mrs. Burton was going through hard times because she believed she was not giving her daughter a normal childhood. She was concerned about the effects her employment may have on her daughter. She felt restricted by her paid work commitments, which made it difficult to give her daughter the same kind of childhood that she herself received.

Her career as a university lecturer had been her topmost priority. She also enjoyed this work very much and described the benefits of her employment in terms of self worth and interaction with other people that had become a way of life for her: 'Just operating in the world outside the home and it just isn't me being at home all the time because I was bored.' However, her problem emerged as a result of her desire to spend time with her daughter and have a successful career.

Mrs. Giles worked in the family business that was mainly managed by her husband. She recalled the day her husband was left by the other partner to run a business on his own without a certificate. She had to give him all the support she could so that he could get the required skills and start all over again: 'I helped him with the study; I would drive down to another town about 100 km and I would sit out in the car with our son while he was in the class or doing his exam.'

As a mother she wanted to give her children the same sort of attention and care that she received from her own mother. She believed that giving small treats to children was necessary for a normal childhood.

> Mrs. Giles: The other day I didn't go to tennis because I felt guilty because there hasn't been spare time and I hadn't caught up with the things at home. I hadn't had any baked cookies for the kids. I felt that was some thing that was done for me as a child which I wanted to do and I felt I should be doing that.

She felt better when she baked biscuits for the children. She wished to make her home comfortable for her husband and children. However, she did not have the time and energy to be able to do all the things she did before she became involved in the family business.

Mrs. Drummond combined paid work and family responsibilities. Although she started paid work for 'self development' she wanted to maintain a happy and stable environment in her family. She had always wanted to make her home a place where the family had security, love and comfort.

> Mrs. Drummond: My mum was a very very warm person and I know that I

loved that feeling. I just love the security of the family...I mean...I am just wrapped in the security and warmth and family life and I am proud to do that. When I was a child I used to hate that if I didn't have it.

She never had time to herself so that she could sit down with a cup of coffee. She wished to have more control over the planning and organisation of her household work: 'I feel normal families have a routine and I feel we should try and get one.' On the other hand she knew with a rigid routine it may not be possible to create the type of family atmosphere she wished.

'It is not impossible but very very difficult'   Mrs. Simmons was a successful working mother. She had continued in paid work throughout her child-bearing years. She believed that even if the mother is employed full-time the family can have a normal life. However, the difference would be that the children would be brought up by a different set of rules compared to the situation where the mother was home on a full-time basis.

After marriage, when she had her first child, she had continued her studies. She wished to continue and complete her studies even during the toughest times.

Mrs. Simmons: It is not impossible to have children and then go back but very very difficult. It was even harder when I was on maternity leave because it is very difficult to work when you are home with a little baby. It is not impossible...well some people may find it easy but I found it very difficult...but I knew I was going back.

She had no regrets about the choice she had made during her child-bearing years. Apart from the financial benefits, she found her career as a scientist intellectually stimulating and personally rewarding. Because she was a career woman she gained her satisfaction mainly from her career. She felt their family home was a place they had to stay and the household work was a means of meeting their basic needs. She shared the household work almost equally with her husband and regarded it as non-rewarding.

'I am earning my own income'   Mrs. Stone was employed part-time and came home before her two boys arrived from school. Managing part-time employment and family was fairly easy for her because she treated her paid work and family separately. She confessed that most of her friends thought she was very lucky because her husband helped her with the household work. She felt her employment situation was an ideal one because she was financially independent as well as being home on time to take care of other important duties. She believed she could not have had a better arrangement.

> Mrs. Stone: When children come home they can't wait to tell you all about their day. They are so pent-up and that's when they need you to talk to and then you got to be there.

She believed being there for her children when they needed her was her utmost priority. She also believed that having to beg one's husband for money for a 'hair cut' can lead to non-employed wives' guilt. She felt fortunate for not having to go through this because she was earning her own income.

Mrs. Broom had always been employed because she liked to keep herself occupied with things outside the home. Although the nature of her paid work was similar to that of household work, it was recognised differently and valued more.

> Mrs. Broom: I think child-rearing is an emotionally and physically demanding job and I don't think that's even acknowledged...in a way I found I might be at work...and give myself a change from here. By having a bit of work there I am earning my own income that gives me a bit of confidence and pride that I work. Sometimes going and working there can be easier than working here all day.

Financial independence was very important to her because, like Mrs. Stone, she believed women who are dependent on their husbands for money are inadequate and limited.

'Working women aren't living through their children's achievements'
Mrs. Jenning was employed part-time. She wanted to extend her hours

to full-time once their three children were in primary school. She believed her children would need her in their early years so therefore she decided to take part-time employment in order to be able to care for them herself. By fitting paid work around her children's needs she believed she could have the best of everything: 'Intuitively I have to say I think it is important for women to be economically independent.'

She was concerned about women's unrecognised contribution towards their families, whereas men's economic contribution in the form of wages and salaries was self evident. Sensing her insecurity, Mr. Jenning reassured her: 'I am formally bringing home the money but there is a lot of work being done at home which is not being paid for and in a way my salary pays for both lots of work and you take charge of spending most of it.' Nevertheless she was convinced that employed women are different because they do much more than housewives.

> Mrs. Jenning: Working women are I feel the women who are going out to work...sort of seeking challenges beyond motherhood and child-care. They have a better perspective of things that they are not so engrossed in their children, and they aren't living through their children's achievements.

Mrs. Jenning had given up her own challenges and had settled half way for the sake of her children. Her dilemma was one of values. She believed good parents were those who had a sense of endurance and commitment to family.

> Mrs. Jenning: We have come to an agreement as to how we would relate to the children and that is as a couple and endure beyond them and relate to children as a unit.

Women and the need for income

'Ours is a financial problem'   Mr. and Mrs. Fielding had set up their home when they got married nine years back. Mrs. Fielding wished her life would unfold like her own mother's. She believed her mother had brought them up 'perfectly' and she wished to follow in her footsteps. Her mother was not employed. She stayed home to look after them. Mrs. Fielding said: 'Ours is a financial problem otherwise I would not have gone to work, I will be home.' She was proud to say that her child-

rearing practices were similar to those of her own mother. She wanted to recreate a family environment that was similar to her family of origin. She believed once their economic situation improves she would be happy to stay home with the children.

Mrs. Sands knew she would have to go back to paid work through economic necessity after her maternity leave. Living in a small town, she knew one has to agree to the employer's terms: 'I don't think women have a choice here...I think you may have more choices in big cities like Sydney but here you have to abide by employer's regulations.' She felt her family situation was not normal because, unlike other mothers, she was a shift worker.

Mrs. Donovan also had to go back to paid work for economic reasons. At the time of interview she was deciding between more money and more time with her children. She was also worried about her children's holiday and after-school care arrangements.

> Mrs. Donovan: Having worked full-time for two weeks till five o'clock trying to think where will the children go I thought they will be shunted around from baby sitter to baby sitter. I don't think it is good because they are only five and seven and need guidance.

She did not feel comfortable leaving the children with a baby sitter for too long. On the other hand she liked her job very much and wished to be employed on a full-time basis. Because her paid work involved interacting with people it was stimulating and interesting and she felt it had helped her become a different person. In addition to being financially independent she was also enjoying the challenges of working with foreign students. She tried to make up for her absence in the family by giving the children her full attention.

> Mrs. Donovan: I know I am tired by evenings...I don't know why I get tired and grumpy...perhaps I don't have the time to devote to some things...I don't know I just find the nights almost in tiredness...really used up.

Mrs Simpson knew she was going back to paid work after each one of her three children were born. Her role as an income earner dominated her other roles. As an employed mother she had organised her household in a particular way to suit school term and holidays. During vacation she became a full-time wife and mother. Her two identities emerged simultaneously a number of times every year. She had to rush around organising a number of things in very little time. Her husband found her 'edgy' and hard to live with during the school term.

> Mr. Simpson: I think non-working wives are easier to live with and they are not tired all the time. When Lyn was on maternity leave or is on holidays everything is lot more relaxed around the house and you don't have to meet the deadlines.

Mrs. Simpson had to go back to paid work for financial reasons after her first child was born. Although she had some reservations in the beginning, she found herself enjoying her teaching career: 'It had benefited me in a lot of ways because you are learning all the time and I am sure there is job satisfaction. It can pull you down sometimes and I think part-time would probably suit me better.' She found the responsibility for three children and a career was an awful load to manage. She was also worried about her youngest child, whose baby sitter was about to leave town. She knew that she had to start looking right away because finding the right person was a great difficulty.

Benefits of paid work for women

'For your own sanity you have to get out and be with people'   Mrs. Harris was employed for 15 years continuously after training as a nurse. She had given up her full-time job in order to start a family. After maternity leave she went back to it a few hours weekly with the intention of increasing it to part-time. Since her paid work was only fractional she found it extremely difficult to adjust at home.

> Mrs. Harris: I think being at home all the time I didn't think I would feel that way...but I think they are long days...and to be on your own...I think it would sound selfish I think for your own sanity you have to get out and be with people and not just the baby.

She did not wish to be employed full-time because she believed she would not have enough time for her son and husband. She believed the part-time situation would suit her because she would be able to fit her job around her family needs and remain in the labour market.

While she was at home she tried to be a perfect mother and doubted her abilities to cope with her son's demands. She often felt disenchanted: 'Going back to work...you sort of enjoy...even though the child-care is a bit of a problem.' Her worries were compounded because she had to investigate child-care on her own. Her husband had left it entirely to her. Without his support she felt dismayed.

Mr. Harris: I left it to Susan because she is at home.
Mrs. Harris: It is more or less if you want to go back, you look for it. To you it didn't even bother...when I said to you the other day...well help me...like you didn't even comment...you only said I don't know of any body...so I investigated it.
Mr. Harris: Well I don't have the time...no way I would have picked and it would have been right.

She was going through a stage when she felt guilty leaving her son with someone else. She often found herself asking if it was all really worth the trouble. She also wanted to maintain her economic independence and believed employed women were lot more confident and assertive by virtue of being financially independent. She was not prepared to give up her years of experience and skills; however, her immediate problem was finding a suitable child-minder.

During the early child-rearing years Mrs. Faldo had given up her career to become a full-time mother to her two children: 'I had just finished my teacher training and felt I had the opportunity to provide a wonderful life to my children.' Her rude awakening was six months after their first son was born.

Mrs. Faldo: I just experienced frustration because that wasn't enough. I knew I was increasingly becoming dependent upon Barney (husband) for stimulation that almost I would bombard him for questions...say something adult to me...I needed to go back for personal fulfilment.
Mr. Faldo: You had to go back for your sanity.

Although she felt restricted by being a full-time mother she faced numerous problems once she went back to paid work. These problems mainly arose from her own guilt that she had to sort out.

Mrs. Faldo: I experienced a feeling of guilt. Should I be doing this? Am I a good mother leaving my child with the childminder? Am I doing the ethical thing?

Some women wished to continue their careers in addition to being mothers and wives. They also looked up to their own mother's ways of bringing them up. They had either put on hold or compromised some of their wishes to keep paid work and family commitments from overlapping.

Mrs. Long was a career woman who once had been a bored housewife. She felt dependent on her husband for everything. She finally decided to go back to school and improve her qualifications. Becoming a professional woman meant a lot to her because it had helped her turn a new leaf.

> Mrs. Long: When I went back to the university I noticed that I became more flexible in my relationship with people and there were more people that I can talk to. I didn't feel I was limited and my vocabulary increased. I was more interested in me and I just felt better about myself...that was the bottom line, the self esteem.

She believed it was very important for women to be financially independent. She considered economic security essential, not only for self development but for future uncertainties. She said she felt safe by knowing that she was capable of taking care of children and herself, should something happen to her husband. It was very important to her that she was a good mother to her children. In her view a good mother was patient and would be willing to make sacrifices for her children.

Mrs. James was a career woman who had continued in paid work throughout her child-bearing years. Rather than being only a housewife and a mother, she felt, she should also work outside the home: 'I am not a home person that's why I got a job and I guess I really get uptight and feel I can't relax not working.' She believed women who stay home as housewives and mothers are confined to a limited world: 'A lot of women centre their lives around their children and their families and they lose their sense of individuality.' She felt it was good for women to be economically independent so that they didn't have to go to their husbands every time they wanted to buy something or get themselves a 'hair cut'. She believed financial security was beneficial especially in the long run, in case of family crisis.

Mrs. James: I don't think it is good to have to be going and begging money all the time which some women do. Their husbands are so tight fisted that they don't think their wives need pocket money and treat it as kids' pocket money. I think it is bad.

In their family housework took a last priority because she knew in order to get it done she would have to 'neglect' her children.

Rigid families

Although the wives in this pattern had similar personal goals as other wives in Trade-off families they extended their roles from being an employee, a mother and a wife to a good home-maker with higher standards in the traditional sense. This maybe a result of their upbringing (Table 6.1). They wished to achieve more than what their resources allowed them and therefore faced several dilemmas.

Conflicting images and needs of women

'There are times when he wants me to be just a housewife'　After maternity leave Mrs. Richards hired a woman to care for her two children. In this way she had the choice to continue her career as well as be a mother. In the beginning she found it difficult to cope with being a mother on a full-time basis. However, she knew it was a temporary situation because once her maternity leave was over she was going to return to her paid work.

Mr. Richards: It was always your intention to go back to work.
Mrs. Richards: Yes...it's something I always wanted to do.
Mr. Richards: Superannuation (laughs).

As an employed mother she felt her priorities would have to be different from non-employed mother who has the time and energy for family responsibilities. By being a teacher in the same school with her children she had the satisfaction of being close to them. But she pointed out: 'Until recently teaching was a fairly good job for a mother, the hours were good, but the pressures at the moment are great.' Because of the changing employment conditions she had to spend more time there, which directly affected her time with her family.

Their household operated differently during school term and during holidays. During the school term she managed to keep only a simple routine with the help of her husband. Her husband and children were aware of the problems that she faced being a teacher and therefore knew about her limited time and energy. Mr. Richards said: 'If Nina was dependent on me then my expectations would be different and I wouldn't have to do any housework.' Mrs. Richards acknowledged her husband's expectations but also knew that he also wanted her to be an 'interesting' partner as well: 'There are times when he wants me to be just a housewife but then again he would be bored too, with someone who is housebound, cooked and cleaned.' She felt it was a compromise between having the luxury of two incomes and having to help with the household work.

Although the money Mrs. Short earned caring for the aged was not very much, it gave her the confidence of making a contribution to the family income. Although the type of work she performed was not very satisfying for her it had changed the way she felt about herself.

> Mrs. Short: It has added a bit of quality from a housewife to working mum and because I haven't been home all day grinding away...not dull as I was either...you know.

Away from household work she enjoyed time with people who valued her as a worker and depended on her for care. She felt financially secure because of her additional income. As much as she tried to settle in her job, her husband and children reminded her of her family obligations.

> Mr. Short: I am not sure whether the youngest would agree with that and the next oldest one...I think they miss their mum especially this one (looks at the youngest son). Sometimes he cries when Kate goes to work and often says when is mum coming back?

Mrs. Short was in the process of reconstructing her image as an employed wife and mother but her husband continued to remind her of her duties as a mother. Ever since she had started paid work she felt she was changing for the better: 'Working has helped me step out of the whole thinking that I was getting old and stuck in the house unemployed. My confidence has been increased and I think I made an improvement in myself and the children respect me for it.' By earning an income she valued herself more than when she did not.

'Working makes my mind much better' Mrs. Mason had stopped paid work in order to start a family. As soon as both her boys had started pre-school she took part-time employment and at the time of the interview she was employed full-time. Although she balanced four roles simultaneously her paid work role was primary, while being a wife and mother and a home-maker took second and third priority respectively.

When Mrs. Mason took a break from paid work for child-bearing she thought she would go back part-time once her children were in school. However, when the opportunity arrived she only had the option of full-time employment. She believed if she let this opportunity go by she would not be able to secure another position.

> Mrs. Mason: I always thought I would go back to work when the children were in the primary but when the cherry was there I felt I had to take it because you only get one bite of the cherry.

Earning an income was very important to her so she did not let this opportunity go by. She felt women should be economically independent in order to live happily: 'I wouldn't like to be dependent, I like to think I have got my own money for things like getting a hair cut or something.' Being able to spend her own money was symbolic for her independence.

Mrs. Mason benefited from her job financially and personally because she felt she was doing something much more valuable than just staying home: 'Working makes my mind much better because you are not sitting at home watching the soapies, watching videos or looking out whether the washing is going to get wet.' As a nurse her job involved challenge and on the spot decision making.

As an employed person she valued her spouse role and mother role much more than her housewife role. She was more concerned about maintaining the identity of a good employee and a good employed mother. She tried not to fuss too much about household chores because she knew it was a never-ending job: 'I guess when I've cleaned up the house I'd say gee that looks good but the rewards are short-lived and I have to do it again.'

'Now the mother is busy and doesn't have the time' Mrs. Black was

employed part-time and used substitute child-care for her children. She was in a transition phase of rediscovering her identity as an employed person, as she juggled mothering, paid work and home-making. With three children under eight the responsibilities sometimes became overwhelming. She was torn between wanting to enjoy her paid work and having to care for children and meet household needs.

Her children's needs increased when they entered school as they had to be driven to various training centres to learn to play sport and swim and so on. She could not enjoy her paid work because her family commitments were too important to be considered secondary or neglected. Her household work and family responsibilities overwhelmed her desire to escape for a few days: 'Lying on the beach...just a few days without the kids getting in the way...just a break...not just a couple of hours but a couple of days.'

Her claim for 'time alone' was her way of coming to terms with her different roles. This was not because she did not wish to continue fulfilling her contradictory roles but to step back and evaluate what she was up against. At the time of this study she was far too involved with her family roles to increase her paid work as a laboratory assistant.

> Mrs. Black: I know it is not possible but just two days...where you don't have to worry about the whole time. So that when you went out you didn't have to worry about them tripping over and hurting and skinning a knee and falling in the water and that they didn't fight.

In an effort to enjoy her identity as an employed mother she was slowly relinquishing some of her mothering duties to a substitute carer. She said her youngest, a two year old, loved her baby sitter and had become attached to her. Knowing that her daughter got on well with her baby sitter Mrs. Black felt relieved and less guilty.

She was also concerned about having to wait a long time before resuming full-time paid work. Her qualifications would be out of date and it would be extremely difficult to secure a full-time job: 'I can talk to Henry (husband) about other than the children and you need that otherwise you are sitting home eating chocolates.'

Given the amount of time available for housekeeping her home-maker role became a last priority. This was for pragmatic reasons. First, she did not have the time to perform household work on a regular basis, and second she felt performing the repetitious chores was a waste of time: 'I wish I had the money to pay someone to do the ironing and things like that and even if I don't do it and I say it doesn't bother me, in the back of my mind I know it is not right and I should be able to do these things.'

Although Mrs. Ferguson was an income earner she lacked financial independence because of their financial commitments. She was making a huge contribution towards the family income but felt bad because she did not have any money for herself.

> Mrs. Ferguson: For me all the money goes into buying things or some payment comes in and I don't get a cent out of it at times and you tend to think why there isn't any money left? Why can't I go and buy pizza for lunch or a new dress or even something small?

By earning money she felt she was playing an important role in their marriage partnership, but she also found satisfaction in being a good mother and a home-maker. When asked how she felt about reversing their roles it appeared she valued her role in the traditional sense.

> Mrs. Ferguson: I enjoy the work I do but I prefer Ricky (husband) to go and earn the money. I think because I like being at home a part-time job is ideal.

Mr. Ferguson felt if his wife was employed full-time then their children would suffer. Mrs. Ferguson admitted that children needed their parents, not only for the basic necessities but also for overall development: 'People don't have enough time these days not even for parenting.' She felt she was doing the right thing by being employed part-time and coming home before the children arrived home from school.

Mrs. Kerrington was employed part-time to have other interests outside the household. She perceived her main role as a wife and mother, and a home-maker. Although she dreaded the household work she enjoyed being at home. She preferred part-time paid work because she believed the children needed her when they came home from school. She recalled her own mother who did not engage in employment but looked after them: 'Now the mother is busy and doesn't have the time and is always rushing.' A mother who was employed full-time was perceived as 'rushed' because she had less time for her children.

97

Mrs. Kerrington's main concern was their teenage children and their welfare. She believed children have different expectations compared to when she was growing up.

> Mrs. Kerrington: Love is not everything...I would have thought it is but it is not...you maybe loving but they push you away...and they don't want that...they really do...you know it's got to be a balance...you got to keep your distance...lots of love and understanding.

Mrs. Davidson was employed part-time. She fitted her job around her family's needs. She had always done this in order to be with her three children: 'The nuclear family in Australia is in a disaster because in order to become independent we have lost contact with the relatives.' She was antagonistic towards mothers who were employed full-time and left their children in the care of someone else. She doubted the substitute carer's responsibilities.

> Mrs. Davidson: Our next door neighbours have someone who comes in and look after the children. Now that is virtually a stranger and living with the children say six or seven hours a day and five days a week and they don't know what sort of values they have...it is the young people who are doing the looking after and maybe they don't have the same morals that you have and therefore the children are a little bit mixed-up.

Mrs. Davidson perceived a good mother to be someone who checked the behaviour of her children because the children continually tested her to define the boundaries.

Some women in Rigid families wished to have it all. They wanted to be financially independent, good wives and mothers, as well as good home-makers. They had higher personal goals, expanded their roles beyond their capacities and tried to keep up with their own mothers' higher standards of doing things. As a result of having placed too many demands on themselves with fewer resources to fulfil them they continually faced dilemmas.

'She is quite irrational about it actually...the kids are never going to starve' During the period when Mrs. White left the labour force to start a family she took music classes that benefited others and rewarded her financially and personally. Being committed to mothering and to her

music she worked out a situation in which she could combine family and music classes at her own home. She believed she was fortunate to have the choice to continue her passion and still be with her children.

> Mrs. White: I started teaching music at my place because it fitted around the needs of the family and I had something to do for myself. Then I went to teach at school as well. It makes you gain your self esteem and you are happier. I like to help the community and also you make money that way.
> Mr. White: It makes you a more interesting person.

Although her husband supported her decision to go back to paid work she found herself facing several problems. Once she started teaching in a school in addition to her evening music classes, she came under the burden of contradicting responsibilities. She continued to bear the responsibilities but felt torn between her role of a mother and a wife as well as being an efficient music teacher. She no longer had the time or the energy to be the mother she once was or to provide the same kind of care and nurturing. Her new role of an employed wife and mother required some changes in the family.

She confided: 'You probably have lowered standards of housework, have more or less take out meals, and when you do make them it is not so called nutritious as your mum might have considered it because you use a lot more convenient items.' She felt she did not have a choice but adapt to the unconventional ways of caring for the family in order to combine her paid work and family commitments.

> Mrs. White: I feel guilty in mind but I don't think Ray (husband) worries, which is excellent but I certainly feel that way.
> Mr. White: Sometimes she is quite irrational about it actually. She gets it in her head that we are not going to eat out for a week and on the other times she might not care.

She felt a mother's employment had some effect on children: 'In some ways it is harmful for them because you don't have as much time to give, you know the times when they need help with homework and you are off to paid work and you are off to meetings and you feel awful about it.' At the same time she believed she was a positive role model for her children and they respected her not only as a mother but as a career person.

At the time of going back to paid work after children Mrs. Fields felt disadvantaged because the job structure did not have a part-time or a job sharing scheme. She felt she had no choice but to take on a full-time job in order to accept the opportunity of re-entering employment.

> Mrs Fields: At the time Johnny (son) was very young I was in another town working and Jerry (husband) had to partly raise him...he had to be a mother. I absolutely hated it because I felt very guilty about it. I also knew in this environment if I didn't go and seek work I may never get work.

She resented the idea of being employed full-time, as her youngest was only a baby. She felt she was not meeting her responsibilities by passing her duties on to her husband. She also took a keen interest in the meals she provided to her family. By cooking a healthy and tasty meal she felt better in herself as a mother and wife: 'We are always trying to make a home that's more pleasant and a home that they can look back and say we had a good home life and things weren't always a chaos because mum worked.'

Having been brought up by a full-time mother, she tried to recreate the same intimacy in her own family. However, by being unable to live up to her own ideals she felt helpless and frustrated. She felt torn between her desire to give the best of her abilities to her family and having to rationalise and accept her limitations.

> Mrs. Fields: For Jerry the most important thing is that I am happy and relaxed but being a woman it's not easy to think this way.
>
> Mr. Fields: Well the kids are never going to starve...but Stacy is never going to be happy if there isn't a three course meal on the table every now and then...it doesn't matter they'll get fed.

Her desire to provide a good home life meant she had to maintain higher household work standards and keep her home spotlessly clean. Maintaining a higher degree of cleanliness gave her the satisfaction of being a good home-maker. She valued other people's opinion of her and therefore regulated their visits when her home was not presentable. To save herself of an embarrassment she politely asked: 'Don't visit us, our house is messy.'

'I found I was quietly going round the twist'   Mrs. Hope had gone

back to paid work against her husband's wishes. During child-bearing she found being a mother and a housewife was not like living a full life: 'Being a housewife I was very bored, I felt inadequate, like I wasn't contributing to the family at all.'

By not contributing economically to the family she felt dependent on her husband for money, friendship and companionship. She recalled the days when she felt stranded in a house full of children.

> Mrs. Hope: I was very dependent on him (husband) so when he got home I followed him around to talk to and wanted to be with him. So because of boredom, feeling of ups and downs with three kids to look after...yes...I still felt inadequate.

Now having gone back to paid work for 'life beyond the four walls' she was forever trying to demonstrate her commitment to her family. She explained that ever since she started to earn an income their standard of living had improved, they had renovated their family home and had acquired more furniture.

She said her family values were traditional and respectable. Because of her endurance and commitment to her husband and children, she believed her involvement in the labour force would not badly affect her family. She continued to perform her duties as a wife and mother and made sure the household remained her responsibility. She further strengthened her argument for family commitments: 'That's the way I have been brought up, looking at my parents.'

She preserved her image of a 'good mother' by comparing her child-rearing practices with those of other people. She believed good parenting can be achieved by bringing up children with discipline.

> Mrs. Hope: I don't believe in a lot of the modern ways of doing things. I like the way I was brought up...I was brought up with morals and discipline. When I ask my children to do something for me I feel that they have to do it. That's what discipline is.

Raising her children to help around the house was a value Mrs. Hope associated with good mothering.

Mrs. Turnbull was a career woman for many years before getting married and having children. After her first son was born she gave up paid work to be a mother on a full-time basis. However, she found she was unsuitable for this role, missing contact with her friends and colleagues. Her efforts to going back to part-time employment were shattered when she learned the job structure did not have that flexibility. She had no choice but to stay with her son or go back to full-time employment. As a mother she felt she had to stay with her baby and decided against being employed full-time.

In the process of becoming a mother she encountered several difficulties. First, she did not knew how to cope with her son who cried most of the time. Second, her husband worked for long hours and did not give her much support, and third, she was living in small rented accommodation which she found was caving in on her. She recalled her mothering experiences.

> Mrs. Turnbull: I just found that I was quietly going round the twist...just couldn't cope...this blob would scream at me, didn't speak to me and nothing I felt I could do right.

A baby who did not interact with her as an adult was perceived as a 'blob', a simple form of mass. Mrs. Turnbull was used to having activities in her day but now she experienced frustration. Her identity of 'just a mother' clashed with her employed friends' image as well. Although they sympathised with her they did not spend any more time with her and her baby than they had to: 'A lot of my friends worked and they didn't have children and they weren't sympathetic to going to lunch with me...they would suddenly say oops got to get back.'

She explained that her dissatisfaction was not so much with her new role as a mother but with having to lose the status of an employed person.

> Mrs. Turnbull: The benefit of being employed makes you feel the value of being needed...even though they pay you to be needed. Being employed satisfied me whereas the need of a child wasn't enough for me or the right kind of need...maybe I am different.

She found that part-time employment was the right choice because she could not bear being at home full-time.

Employed women and financial independence

'Women who are financially independent are confident' Mrs. Turner

had sad memories from her previous marriage. She believed she was not treated properly because she was not earning an income and therefore she accounted for every cent she spent. Her marriage was not fulfilling because of her unequal status in the marriage partnership. She rebuilt herself by remarrying and earning an income. This time she was determined to remain financially independent: 'Women who are financially independent are confident and like I don't have to ask for money and I am independent to spend on what and whom I like.' Being financially independent, Mrs. Turner regained self confidence and self worth. However, this did not lead to role sharing with her partner. Having experienced one troubled marriage she felt she was not going to press her husband to renegotiate their role-relationship. When asked about their household work arrangements she explained it was not worth causing a conflict.

Mrs. Brown believed she was fortunate to have the choice to do paid work part-time and continue her teaching career. She insisted that there was no such thing as an ideal motherhood that came naturally to women.

> Mrs. Brown: I don't think there is such a thing as a good mother...well not an ideal one...I don't know what makes a good mother. I had never nursed a new born baby and when I had mine...I said oh God...I hate it...even the second one. I think a good mother is one who provides all basic things and checking their temper when you feel like throwing them out of the window sometimes...you have to work at being a parent.

Over the last few years she had learned to be loving and caring for someone whom she could not relate to in the beginning. She believed part of the reason for her success in parenting was the fact that she continued in paid work part-time and therefore did not go through a sudden change in status. She knew that once her second baby was weaned she would increase her hours to full-time.

As a career mother she was concerned about preserving her status in the family once her two boys were older. She was determined to portray herself as an employed rather than a full-time mother.

> Mrs. Brown: I have thought about this before that I will continue to work in their growing years and I don't want them to see me as the 'home-maker' without acknowledging that I go to work as well. I don't want them to think that I am doing everything...I mean I won't get over board.

103

It was important for her to establish her identity as a person who could do more important and challenging things than her housework.

Mrs. Wills had become a successful business woman although she had had a period of being at home full-time. When they had first moved to this town to set up business her husband had lost his job as a carpenter and now employed in their family business of organic foods which was predominantly managed by his wife. He was not happy about this arrangement because he wanted her to be a traditional wife and mother.

> Mr. Wills: As women get paid jobs there is no longer the sort of feeling of dependence to the male and if there is a problem in the family the male will say: 'Oh blow this, I have got enough I am off', now I think probably just as likely the other way around the woman knows that she can stand on her two feet.

He felt his wife's economic independence had become a thorn in their relationship. He felt he did not have much say in the daily running of the household and other important family decisions. On the other hand, Mrs. Wills was determined to continue things the way they were not so much for financial reason but self-fulfilment.

> Mrs. Wills: The business has helped me spiritually in the sense that I had been exposed to other people's ideas, I had led a very closed life before I had opened the shop because I had very little contact with people.

She believed a family was a unit of reciprocity so she should not be the only one to care for other members: 'I don't think one person should wait on the rest of the family and I think that's stupid but yet a lot of us do it for a lot of years.' Even though her husband still preferred for a wife who stayed home and looked after them, there was no turning back for her: 'I think a woman who is dependent on her husband is far more subservient and part of the agreement is that she looks after him.'

Conclusions

Financial security was of equal importance to wives in both Trade-off and Rigid families. This can be observed from Table 6.1, as having a 'hair cut' with one's own money was valued highly. Wives who had left the work force for child-rearing found rejoining the labour market on a full-time basis very difficult. Their guilt mainly resulted from their attachment to their children, and home-making standards that they had developed while staying home. When they tried to compromise on those standards they felt as if they were betraying their husbands and children. On the other hand, the wives who knew they were going back to paid work after maternity leave faced fewer problems and resumed their contributor and employed mother roles relatively easily.

Wives who were career-oriented and detached from their family roles felt less guilty about poor household work standards or leaving their children in full-time child-care. They achieved personal satisfaction and self esteem from paid work related successes and considered their mothering role important but not the only thing in their lives. They also maintained their economic independence and did not let themselves to be taken for granted by other members of the family.

In the process of becoming employed wives and mothers, all women experienced guilt at some stage or the other. The only difference was in the way they managed role overload, and dealt with their dilemmas and in the amount of support they received from their partners. Wives who felt they would not be able to cope had put their full-time job options on hold until their children were older and self sufficient.

A significant contrast can be observed from how wives defined their present situation in Trade-off families and Rigid families. While the wives in Rigid families wished to achieve their personal goals of being 'career women', 'good wives and mothers' as well as 'good home-makers', the wives in Trade-off families renegotiated their priorities in a way that they could manage paid work and family fairly comfortably. In other words, they did not commit themselves to any role in particular.

By following rule 6 in Figure 3.3 in Chapter 3, Trade-off families realistically handled their personal goals and role definitions and therefore were able to manage their dilemmas effectively. In contrast, the wives from Rigid families were unrealistic in handling their personal goals and role definitions and therefore were unable to manage their dilemmas effectively. Overall it could be concluded that all women were still in the ongoing process of becoming successful employed wives and mothers.

7 Are the Perceptions of Ground Rules and of Self and Other, Flexible or Inflexible?

In this chapter I discuss couples' attitudes towards their paid work and family roles and the extent to which they bargain their responsibilities to suit their three-job situation. I explore husbands' and wives' perceptions of their own and their partner's family roles (household division of labour) and the extent to which these are unconventional or viriarchal. I do this by examining: 1) who takes on the responsibility and allocates chores in the household; 2) who does what and how much around the household; and 3) who takes charge and how they react if the going gets tough in the household.

Husbands and wives in families under the Trade-off model had flexible perceptions of 'own roles' and 'partner's roles', as well as the ground rules of their household. In contrast, couples under the Rigid model had inflexible perceptions of ground rules and of 'self' and 'other' roles. It can be claimed that families under the Trade-off model differed from families under the Rigid model with reference to rule 7 in Figure 3.3. This is in line with the differences observed in husbands' and wives' perceptions of 'household ground rules' and of 'own roles' and 'partner's roles' (Tables 7.1 and 7.2). Husbands and wives from Trade-off families (Table 7.1 and 7.2) have mutual, flexible and egalitarian attitudes towards gender roles, while the wives and particularly husbands, from Rigid families have resisting, inflexible and viriarchal attitudes. This maybe seen as a contributing factor to effective (M) or ineffective (P) management of household work contradictions in Figure 3.3. The points to observe in Tables 7.1 and

7.2 are the extreme contrasts between the utterances of husbands and wives in Rigid families and Trade-off families.

Table 7.1 Husband's Perceptions of Self/Identity, Own Roles, Partner's Identity, Partner's Roles, and Negotiation Pattern

Family Model (No)	Family Name	Self/Identity	Self Roles	Partner's Identity	Partner's Role	Negotiation Pattern
Trade-Off (20)	Burton	-Part-time work for both three days a week would be better	- I do house work because it needs doing	-She does more than I do	-She is particular about cleaning (+)	-We talk about it and I usually give in
	Knight	-I am quite happy to do the ironing	- I do house work because it needs doing	-She can step into my role	-She hasn't nagged (+)	-If she hates something then I'll do it
	Giles	-I am on call 24 hrs a day	- I like gardening	-She stood by me	-She has hired help (+)	
	Simmons	-I don't mind working part-time and doing house work	- I like to plan the chores and do them	-She has her own chores	-She has her career (+)	
	Stone	-I wish I didn't have to work night shifts	- I am not picky or a stressful person	-She works part-time to be with the kids	-She does the indoor chores	-When I am working 60 hours/week it has to be negotiated
	Broom	-I think two part-time jobs would be good	- I had to learn to do the house work and the parenting	-I hate how she hangs clothes on the line	-She does the indoor chores	-I think negotiation is an ongoing thing
	Faldo	-I make breakfast and pack the dishwasher		-She cooks the main meals		-We hardly talked about it, it just happened

107

Long	-I think the man should be the provider	-I give in	-She has ironed if I am late and tired	-She reminds me about chores to the point of nagging	-If one of us gets crazy with work it is a signal to the other
Jenning	-I have always cleaned the bathroom	-I get stressed if she gets stressed	-She drives the car she knows what is wrong with it	-I don't contradict her responsibilities	
Feilding	-I was never a home bound	-I used to leave the house when there was a problem	-I appreciate what she does	-If I was earning enough she wouldn't have to work	
Simpson	-I wish my job was more flexible	-I do all the yard work	-Her income helps the family	-She cooks better when she is not working	-There are a few jobs we both go past
Sands	-I do some of the ironing and a lot of cooking	-I don't mind role reversal	-She is very efficient	-She does most of the housework	-I will give subtle and not so subtle hints
Drummond	-I take care of the outside things	-I wouldn't mind who provides for the family	-She always cooks		
Harris	-If I have to stay home I can cope	-I have come home and started the dinner	-She can earn more than me		-You start doing the most important jobs
Donovan	-If I was out of work then she can provide	-I have been ironing since primary school			
James	-I don't mind washing or hanging but I won't iron	-I like to cook			

108

Rigid (14)	Richards	-It is my job to provide for others	-I do my chores on a need's basis	-She sees the dirt first	-I like her to come home at a sensible hour (-)	-We sort out the priorities and then negotiate
	Short	-I don't have the final say I feel uneasy for not pulling my end	-I help her	-Kids miss her	-She takes the obligation and the responsibility for the house (-)	
	Mason	-We can survive on my income	-I do the outdoor work	-She works for above and beyond		
	Black	-I am not a very good cook and I don't enjoy cooking	-I have changed the dirty nappies	-She worked full-time before we had the children	-She is equipped to breast feed (-)	-She hates ironing so I do it and do it my way
	Ferguson	-I should be able to provide for my family	-I don't mind being a house husband	-She told me ironing is not a man's job	-She doesn't let me do indoor chores (-)	
	Kerrington	-I am quite content to be the major provider	-I enjoy cooking	-She works part-time	-She has been the main provider in the past	-We usually have an argument about it
	Davidson	-In our society husband is the main provider	-It was equal sharing before the kids			
	White	-I work for a living	-I don't worry about the meals	-Her job is a fun doing	-She worries too much (-)	
	Fields	-I help her	-I am not a gardener	-Her income is essential	-She is fussy about the meals (-)	
	Hope	-I am the boss	-I do the outside work	-I didn't want her to work	-She is the home maker (-)	

109

Turner	-I work Mon. to Sat.	-I will do the chores if she can't or if I have to	-She pressures me	-She should do the housework (-)	-We talk about it and make other people feel guilty and we go yelling and screaming
Turnbull	-I work and study	-I tend to like to keep the place tidy a little bit	-She is the organiser	-She is messy (-)	-The most alert asks the other and then the responsibility or the choice is put upon the other
Brown	- I should be the breadwinner	-My family was surprised how much I do for the children	-The female is responsible for house work	-I don't nag her, she nags me (-)	-I give in to keep the peace
Wills	-I am the subservient male	-The male should provide the income	-She is the heroine	-The wife should take care of the house (-)	-No chance of sitting and watching TV. Not with madam over there giving orders

Table 7.2 Wife's Perceptions of Self/Identity, Own Roles, Partner's Identity, Partner's Roles, and Negotiation Pattern

Family Model (No)	Family Name	Self/Identity	Self Roles	Partner's Identity	Partner's Role	Negotiation Pattern
Trade-Off (20)	Burton	-I think part-time work for both would be better	- I am the one who does the kitchen floor	-He was very good when we reversed roles	-He does the washing up (+)	-We talk about it
	Knight	-I didn't work when children were little	- I think the mother has something special to offer to children	-He has taken the ironing off my hands	-He still helped me when I wasn't working (+)	-He said you seem to be spending a lot of time ironing why don't I try it
	Giles	-I like to think the male is the provider	- I help him in the business	-He is on call 24 hrs a day		-He said get someone to do the ironing and the house work
	Simmons	-I think provider role should be equally shared	-I am a successful scientist with his support	-He shares housework with me		-We plan things and stick to the plan
	Stone	-I work part-time to be with the children	-I am home before kids come from school	-He works on shifts	-I sometimes have to remind him things	
	Broom	-I think provider role should be shared with two part-time jobs	-I like to find a job that satisfies me	-I had to domesticate him	-He doesn't mind the housework (+)	-Life is a continuous struggle and you got to keep on negotiating
	Faldo	-I think provider role should be a shared responsibility	-If you share the earning then home should be shared	-He is observant and helps me out when I get overworked	-He complements me (+)	

111

Long	-I like to share the provider role	-I don't get a great of satisfaction from doing the house work	-He is sexist	-I have to remind him his chores (-)	-We seem to negotiate a balance quite often
Jenning	-Being home full-time is not going to satisfy me	-I do the heavy work	-He has been good with child care and changing nappies	-He can see the gaps now (+)	-We discussed and came to an agreement about doing certain chores
Feilding	-I wouldn't like to be the breadwinner	-I miss being home	-His paid work is cut down because of the drought	-He can't manage on his own (-)	
Simpson	-I think part-time work would probably suit me	-I bring home work every night	-He helps me prepare for the next morning	-He is not much of a cook (-)	
Sands	-I work on shifts	-I try to finish housework before he gets home	-He cooks the meals	-He does all the indoor cleaning (+)	
Drummond	- I found it difficult to look after a baby so I work	-I find a lack of control over the environment (household)	-He is quite happy to stay at home	-He doesn't see the housework as I do (-)	
Harris	-I think the husband should provide	-I believe the mother does a better job of bringing up little babies	-He is the cook	-He takes our son away when I am busy (+)	
Donovan	-I am an outdoor person	-I think part-time work is better when children are young	-He has a lot of physical exertion with building work	-He does the ironing (+)	

112

	James	-I needed a job because I am not a home person	-I am not a good home maker	-He won't iron		
Rigid (14)	Richards	-I have to be highly organised	-If someone comes to our house and it isn't tidy I feel responsible	-If we have to choose it would be his role to provide for us	-He helps but I don't like the way he does it (-)	
	Short	-I have to fit everything around his study time table	-If I was working full-time I wouldn't have time for anybody	-We are here for his study	-The more I nagged the less he wanted to do chores (-)	
	Mason	-I'd rather be out at work than waiting for the washing to dry	-I do everything	-I think he should do his own paper work, not me	-To avoid the conflict I just pay the bills for him (-)	
	Black	-I like to use my ability and work is good for my brain	-When kids are at school I will work full-time	-He can't cook	-He used to change baby's nappies for me (+)	
	Ferguson	-I work for money	-I don't like mowing the lawn	-I prefer if he earn the money	-He isn't motivated to do man's chores (-)	
	Kerrington	-I think it is wife's role to keep the house	-I enjoy being at home but I don't like the house work	-I am happy with him being the provider	-He has to understand kids (-)	It is not something that is you sit down and talk about it
	Davidson	-I want secure and regular work	-I don't find any real rewards doing the housework	-I don't think he will cope with being a house husband		

113

White	-I make less money	-I think of the house as my responsibility	-He can stand a higher level of mess	-I wish he can come home and help me with dinner (-)	-May be I shouldn't be grizzling about him not coming home to help
Field	-I love working and being around people	-I think the mother should do the house work and look after the children	-He doesn't mind the lowered standards	-I keep on reminding him to dig the garden (-)	-I have to remind him all the time
Hope	-I work to get away from everything	-I am happy with the indoor-outdoor arrangement	-He was a saviour when kids were young	-He does the outdoor more	
Turner	-I don't have to ask for money	-If things require strength I can't do them	-He comes home and complains he is tired	-He won't do women's work (-)	
Turnbull	-I don't mind if the house isn't tidy	-House work is not totally my responsibility	-He lives here too	-He doesn't think that we go and eat at night (-)	
Brown	-I should be working full-time once I get a little mobile (stop feeding)	-We had reversed our roles when the first one was born	-He should be working part-time and looking after son as I earn more	-I don't like the way he pegs clothes (-)	
Wills	-I used to think it was right for the man to earn	-I prefer to be the man myself	-I am wasting energy asking him		-I have to prod to get things done

Trade-off families

Families under this model wished to achieve ways in which they could handle paid work and family responsibilities properly. They perceived these responsibilities objectively, and continually tried to negotiate and bend the ground rules in search of efficiency. This was possible because both partners were compromising and fairly flexible and less fussy about their beliefs as to how things should be done in the household.

'Reading the other partner' Mr. and Mrs. Burton rationalised that in an ideal situation the breadwinner role could be shared. A few months back Mr. Burton had stayed home and cared for their baby. They had reversed their roles because he was looking for employment as he had moved to this town with his wife's new job.

Over the years through task specialisation they had regularly performed some tasks which eventually became their own chores. They had never sat down to discuss the details of their household division of labour, but sort of 'fell into' a kind of unique pattern. Mrs. Burton said: 'We have our own things like Don (husband) will do the washing up and I'll cook and I do all the cleaning in the house.' When asked how they decided their household roles they indicated that a reasonable and fair negotiation continued at all times.

> Mr. Burton: We talk about it...and I usually give in.
> Mrs. Burton: Ah I don't know (laughs)...if I feel strongly about something.
> Mrs. Burton: We are inclined to work a little bit ourselves first and then talk about it. I think there are some things that he gives to me to work out and in that sense I call the shots. I don't know whether we sort of balance out on some things. I think we have a sort of understanding about which things go which way.

Having a sort of 'understanding' between themselves over task allocation implied that they had 'good communication'.

Mr. and Mrs. Knight entered marriage with two jobs but once they started a family they discussed their roles to find a way to best care for them. They believed the mother should be the main carer as Mrs. Knight said: 'Even in the shared duties it is still something that the mother has and it is something special.'

They had negotiated some of the mundane chores in a way that the person who did not mind doing them would be the one to do them. Mr. Knight said: 'I am quite happy to work in the yard and I do the ironing and I am quite happy with that...I don't mind that.' Mrs. Knight confirmed: 'Probably that's one thing I don't like.' Reading the other partner's feelings about certain chores was the basis of their negotiation of household roles. They perceived the household work as something that was there and needed to be done.

Mr. Knight: Sarah hasn't ever nagged me for mowing the lawn as to 'go and mow the lawn'. I do it because it needs doing.

Mrs. Knight: I guess what happened with the ironing would be a classic example. Because I have never relished the thought of ironing and one day you said (looks at Sandy) you seem to spend a lot of time why don't I try it...and I gladly handed it over (laughs) and I never looked back.

Mr. and Mrs. Faldo believed that home-making responsibilities should be shared in order to play the marital roles fairly. Their household division of labour was based on task specialisation. Although their contributions were based on gender they considered it fair and even.

Mr. Faldo: Some things are shared...between the two of us...not including the kids now...and others are not. Typically I make breakfast and typically you make the main meals.

Mrs. Faldo: Yes...because I do more laundry and you do more outside work and sometimes that changes.

Mr. Faldo: In the morning when you are doing the laundry I will be packing the dishwasher...that sort of thing. That has come about...we haven't decided on that...we hardly talked about it...that just always happened.

In their household they did not find the need to keep tabs on other members or regulated each other's chore performance because a feeling of goodwill persisted at all times.

'Get somebody to take pressure off' The Giles had entered marriage with very traditional expectations. Mrs Giles recalled: 'When we initially got married I thought, OK I am going to be at home raising the children and that's going to suit me fine.' But as it turned out her husband went into partnership running a business on his own and she was obliged to help him. Her involvement in the business was not planned or discussed but something that eventuated out of necessity. In the beginning Mrs. Giles found it extremely difficult to cope with the household work and children's responsibilities as well as playing a greater role in the family business.

Mrs. Giles: I can remember a lot of the incidences when there was chaos and I had no outside help. Danny said: 'OK get somebody to take pressure off'...I think it is wonderful.

116

With hired help the household work burden became less, and consequently it became irrelevant.

Household management strategies

'Just follow the routine or no routine' The Simmons were a career-oriented couple who shared their provider and home-maker roles equally. Mrs. Simmons did not interrupt her career during child-bearing. They believed no one partner should be pressured to provide for other family members. They felt an ideal situation would be if both partners do paid work and share child-care and home making responsibility.

Their earning capacities were similar so they shared their household work almost fifty fifty. They had their own duties which they performed spontaneously. They did not wait to be reminded or nagged about their own responsibilities.

> Mrs. Simmons: We have a routine...so we just follow our routine.
> Mr. Simmons: We don't go from a crisis to a crisis situation.

Part of the reason for their lack of attachment to the household work was the fact that they were very much involved with their careers and consequently household work was given last priority.

The Drummonds did not have a rigid perception about who should take on the breadwinner and home-making roles. They said they would not mind either way because it really boils down to the way the couple decides. However, Mrs. Drummond felt that being a full-time mother can be onerous. She found it very difficult to be at home full-time and look after a baby. She finally decided to do paid work part-time.

> Mrs. Drummond: Well I am so much relaxed going off to work it surprises me. The household jobs are 24 hours and 7 days a week and this is like three hours rest from that. Otherwise you just don't get a break from it.

Their household work arrangements resembled a traditional pattern, where Mrs. Drummond performed the indoor chores and her husband did the outdoor chores. They did not follow a strict household routine and only did the chores on a needs basis. In their easy going manner they did not feel the need to engage in any form of negotiation over household work.

117

'Reminding the other partner and giving-in'   Mr. and Mrs. Stone believed that Mr. Stone's single income would not provide everything for the family, especially for their two boys' education. Mr. Stone said: 'There is no pressure on the husband alone to provide for others it is on both partners.' Shifting the pressure off the male to both partners meant that the responsibility had to be shared.

In the beginning they were employed full-time and experienced conflict and unhappiness because Mrs. Stone could not cope with the family demands. Their sense of responsibility towards household management differed considerably.

> Mrs. Stone: I would keep on reminding him if I feel I want him to do something and he doesn't and fed up...(laughs).
> Mr. Stone: I am not picky...I don't bother myself. I am not a stressful person.
> Mrs. Stone: You would let me know sometimes...it depends on your mood.

Mr. and Mrs. Broom believed that ideally a perfect family relationship could be achieved if both partners were employed part-time and shared child-care and home-making duties. Even with their shared household work arrangements they fussed over the way they did some of the chores. Mr. Broom hated the way his wife hung the washing on the line, using too many pegs unnecessarily. He was also aware that she did not approve of his cooking and often criticised him.

> Mrs. Broom: I think it changes you as you get old, some habits are hard to break. If Ken doesn't do something right then I try and change it.
> Mr. Broom: What tends to happen is that you tend to ignore them to the point when somebody says 'you should have done this' or yell 'you didn't do that' or you know...and I usually give in...because there are more reasons in terms of the work. We share the house and the parenting and that sort of stuff. I had more to learn so it was fair enough that I was the person giving in. I wasn't a naturally domesticated sort of a person.

'Giving-in' to his wife's suggestions was not a problem because Mr. Broom did not find it demeaning.

Husbands and wives under this model had somewhat egalitarian perceptions about the breadwinner role. It can be observed from their responses in Table 7.1 that the husbands were more accommodating to

118

their wives' ways of doing things, whereas the wives appeared to acquiesce in the process of working out how best they could retain their domestic role in addition to their paid work responsibilities.

Mr. and Mrs. Long had been married for five years. They had set up a blended family with children from their previous marriages. When asked how they felt about the provider role Mr. Long said: 'Being sexist I still think the man should be the provider.' Mrs. Long had egalitarian views that were influenced by her previous marital experiences: 'Truly I think I had a hard time in the past when I was making money and the man wasn't so I think it should be shared.' She believed that if both partners earned family income then there is some sort of balance and no one feels financially dependent on the other partner.

As far as their household roles were concerned they perceived that their contribution towards household work was fairly equal. They monitored each other, swapped and negotiated with other members when they could not do their own chores. They were not regimented about doing their chores and often reminded each other of their responsibilities.

> Mr. Long: Well she reminds me if I am not doing any of my chores and she nags me...she does all those things.
> Mrs. Long: It's terrible (laughs).
> Mr. Long: She always reminds me of all those things she doesn't want to be doing...she will say OK you want to do that or...and she keeps on to the point of nagging sometimes...and I give in isn't it?
> Mrs. Long: I guess so. I guess I get very verbal if I am not happy.

They felt that negotiation of household roles required people to be good listeners, perceptive, and adaptable to the changes that take place in the family. They saw their home as a haven where members helped each other to deal with pressures and stresses of life. Mr. Long said: 'One has to be protective of one's partner from different rampages whatever society happens to be.'

The Donovans' household division of labour was traditional: each was responsible for either indoor and outdoor chores. Because there were more indoor chores Mr. Donovan helped his wife on a needs basis. Mrs. Donovan boasted that her husband had taken on ironing willingly, but she never knew how he felt about it.

Mr. Donovan: Ironing was legacy of my childhood. It is one of the chores I
had hated. Since primary school I have been doing my own ironing.

Mrs. Donovan: Oh you poor thing, I blame your mother for that (both
laugh).

When Mrs. Donovan arrived home from paid work she often ended up
starting the evening routine because Mr. Donovan worked late in the
evenings. In the past whenever Mrs. Donovan tried to negotiate
household roles there had been a disagreement between them. She
confessed it was not what she asked her husband, but the way she asked
him.

Mrs. Donovan: I will ask you if I am really tired would you mind if you
bathed the kids? I used to sort of nag in inverted commas. If it's why
don't you do that? I found that causing friction in the end.

'Having a go' at each other for no reason depicted the challenges of
being married and the dynamics that entailed in making the marriage
work. Their current task of negotiation was the 'coffee cup' which Mr.
Donovan left in the lounge rather than taking it to the kitchen sink. He
admitted: 'The more Linda (wife) reminds me about the coffee cup the
more it doesn't go to the sink...it is the game people play'. This game of
testing each other's endurance often emerged during the household work
negotiation.

The Sands had reversed their roles when their only son was born, so
Mrs. Sands could earn a higher income while her husband improved his
qualification as well as caring for the baby. They shared household
work to a large extent and did not have a rigid task allocation.

Mr. Sands: If I feel something hasn't been done then I will give subtle and
not so subtle hints to do that. Rene does the same with me, a kind of
reminder.

Their subtle negotiations continued as they both reminded each other
if they were not contributing to an overall balance.

Negotiation of roles

'We came to an agreement'   In the Jenning family two things were
considered essential in the negotiation of the breadwinner role: earning

capacity and life stage. Mrs. Jenning said: 'I feel that if you have children then at least one person should be able to take the time to care for them.' They considered home-making as a 'joint responsibility', irrespective of who takes charge of household chores. They shared the household work and saw some benefit in its performance.

> Mr. Jenning: Nothing is like having it finished. I quite enjoy washing up ...cleaning the bench top whatever it is called surface.
> Mrs. Jenning: I get most rewards from public viewing. Yeah, there is reward in having things looking nice.

Their current negotiation of household division of labour was subtle and 'spontaneous'. They felt responsible and therefore tried to perform their chores as a result of goodwill. This is not to say that they had not engaged in overt negotiations of task allocation in the past.

> Mrs. Jenning: We came to an agreement that it was energy wasting to argue about or discussing. There were times when you decided that it was your job to clean the bathroom and my (her) job to clean the griller.
> Mr. Jenning: I have always cleaned the bathroom. It seems normal to clean the bathroom on a Sunday morning.
> Mrs. Jenning: That you will wash the floor on some days as well. We seem to have taken roles on without any confrontation from me.

With three children under nine and two full-time paid jobs the Simpsons had to negotiate in a number of areas to keep things under control. They had two types of household work patterns: one during the school term and the other in the school holidays.

> Mrs. Simpson: I think when I am working things are shared a lot more down the middle and the division of labour is more even. When I am not working I tend to be a lot more domestic.

They talked about how best they could manage their two paid jobs and an enormous amount of household work. Mr. Simpson took on some chores like making sandwiches, laundry and ironing, and bathing and preparing kids for bed. During weekends he helped even more.

'I wouldn't like to be the breadwinner' Mr. and Mrs. Fielding had to renegotiate their breadwinner role due to harsh agricultural conditions in

which Mr. Fielding was forced to cut down his paid work hours. Because she was temporarily 'filling in' for her husband's breadwinner role, Mrs. Fielding found it extremely difficult to manage the conflicting responsibilities.

> Mrs. Fielding: I wouldn't like to be the breadwinner because I would miss the home and it is so demanding if you go to work also and come home and switch into a different mode. Like I have to catch up on all that I have missed while at work.

They had started their marriage along traditional lines and wished to continue this pattern. Mrs. Fielding considered her paid work 'temporary', and thought renegotiation of their household division of labour was unnecessary and cumbersome.

Mr. and Mrs. Harris differed on who should provide income in a family. Mr. Harris believed a couple should decide on the basis of their earning capacity because in the current economic times one needs to earn a good income to support the family. In his opinion the husband could stay home with the children if his wife had a higher earning capacity. Mrs. Harris: 'I still believe that it is the mother who does a better job in bringing up little babies and taking care of the household.'

> Mrs. Harris: Male and female are suited to certain roles. I feel that the female is really better or more capable for some things...I don't know whether it's just instincts or...but women are capable of sort of handling those sort of situations better than men. I feel it is the husband who is more suited to the wage earner type.

'Kenny won't iron' In the James household both partners were equal providers. The sharing of the breadwinner role had emerged over the last 14 years as they brought their own job to the marriage. Their household division of labour was traditional, but Mrs. James received her husband and children's help on a needs basis. Mrs. James said: 'Housework has to be shared otherwise you will never survive.' Mr. James agreed: 'If both working then you got to share.' It must be noted here that their perceptions of a sharing were in terms of husband helping the wife when and if she needed an extra pair of hands.

Their philosophy was to 'get in and do it' rather than argue about it. They also respected each other's disliking of certain household chores.

122

Mr. James: I don't mind washing or hanging but the only thing I draw the line at is I won't do the ironing.

Mrs. James: Kenny won't iron, needless to say I have got lounge full of ironing at the moment. It gets done eventually.

Although Mr. James disliked ironing it was not his own ironing that was the issue. He said: 'I work outside and I don't need a clean shirt every day.'

Rigid families

Families under this model depicted a somewhat traditional orientation to the provider role. Husbands perceived their wives in the role of a wife and a mother and considered themselves as the breadwinners. Although the wives in families under this model wished to maintain links with the outside world through their paid work they were less than enthusiastic about relinquishing their authority in the domestic sphere.

Traditional division of labour

'Husband outdoor and wife indoor'   With regard to the provider role Mr. and Mrs. Richards never felt the need to sit down and negotiate roles because Mrs. Richards brought her career into the marriage and continued until their first baby was born. Once her maternity leave was over she went back to paid work. Similarly, they had never been in a conflict where they had to deliberate household roles because they spontaneously fell into the 'husband outdoor' and 'wife indoor' pattern. Although Mrs. Richards had been earning a good income they felt that 'ideally' Mr. Richards was the breadwinner in their family.

Mr. Richards: Well let's just talk about ourselves for now...we both worked since we married. When it comes to the crunch and if we had to make the decision about who is to continue working it would be me.

Mrs. Richards: Yes I am quite happy with that.

Mr. Richards: It would be my role, but it has never been that way...Nina has always shared except for maternity leave.

Mrs. Richards: I do agree with Andrew (husband) that it would be his role to provide for us.

Their household division of labour was also based on traditional attitudes. Mr. Richards maintained the yard, both cars, and did other maintenance jobs, and helped his wife in some indoor chores. Although he assisted his wife in such feminine chores they both knew that the ultimate responsibility of maintaining family routine was her area. Being aware of her role Mrs. Richards took on the duties associated with it: 'I suppose it is a social thing isn't it? If someone comes to the house and it isn't tidy I feel responsible for that.' She further agreed that if her husband takes on the outside work then it is understood that she does the inside chores. Mr. Richards corrected his wife by reminding her: 'I do some of the indoor tasks like the bathroom, toilet and the laundry.' However, irrespective of his help the fact remained that it was she who made sure he did his chores. Furthermore, because he was only a helper assisting his busy wife he often forgot to perform his chores.

Mrs. Richards was not financially dependent on her husband. However, she was aware of her husband's expectation of her as a wife and a mother: 'I think you would like me to be your 'little housewife' and have everything prepared for you when you come through that door.'

Mr. and Mrs. Short had been living together for about 10 years. In recent years Mr. Short had given up his paid work to improve his qualifications by taking a degree course. Although he earned a small income his wife was the main income earner in their family. This arrangement had had an effect on Mr. Short's self image.

> Mr. Short: I guess since I haven't been providing since I have been studying...there are two voices inside me, one is that it should be shared and the other is...I feel uneasy about not pulling my end for a number of years.

Although he had the privilege of spending time and nurturing children by virtue of being at home, he yearned for 'masculine' tasks: 'At first this arrangement really worked for me to spend some more time with the children...but I guess that's wearing off and I am feeling that I like to do some physical work.' He believed that it was not natural for men to be involved in home making and nurturing tasks. He felt his image in the family was changing as the children were demanding love and attention and his wife was expecting higher household work standards.

Mr. Short: When I started studying and we had a kind of role reversal I started to feel it wasn't actually healthy for men to spend a lot of or all of their time around children or the house. My guess is that something goes on in there...maybe it is the hormones...a bit of a flip pattern.

This feeling was partially due to his wife's attachment to her traditional role. She said: 'Doing the absolute swap (role reversal) isn't any good for me or for the children as I tend to get automatic and forget what is important.'

They did not have a clear division of household chores because as a man Mr. Short felt it was not his responsibility to take over the household. Mrs. Short was ambivalent because she could neither relinquish her duties nor fulfil them adequately. Mr. Short said: 'Kate still takes the obligation and somehow she has got the responsibility of the house and maybe because of that I don't have that final say which I would have had if I was providing.'

'Her income helps to buy those extras' The Masons had been in paid work prior to starting a family. They had not sat down to decide about the breadwinner and home-maker roles. Mrs. Mason stayed home during child-bearing years and slowly increased her paid work hours to full-time. When asked who should be the provider in the family Mrs. Mason said: 'There are no hard and fast rules, couples can negotiate depending on their particular situation at the time.' However, Mr. Mason believed that the husband's income is the main income whereas wife's income is additional for 'above and beyond'.

Mr. Mason: One can only get an x amount of dollars and you feel you need a bit more either to cope with the situation or adjust that amount and decide not to have a second income and get along. It is between the family. We can survive on my income but her (wife's) income helps to buy more stuff and those extras.

When they first set up a home of their own their household roles emerged along traditional lines as they began gender-based chores right from the start. This pattern strengthened during child-bearing years when Mrs. Mason gave up her job to care for the children. Even though she was employed full-time she still continued to take on the household

125

responsibilities.

'It still boils down to the woman doing more' A number of important factors were considered by Mr. and Mrs. Black in negotiating their roles. Mr. Black said it did not really matter who provided for the family, whereas Mrs. Black believed one has to consider a number of issues: 'It is something that the couple has to decide depending upon the stage of life at the time and if they had young children and if she wants to go back to work.'

Their household roles turned out to be gender-based because of practicality and time availability.

> Mrs. Black: The housework can be shared but perhaps it is the up bringing or if the wife has more expertise in cooking or if you have little children and you are staying at home then you tend to do more of the home making because of the sheer fact that you are there.

Overwhelmed by children's needs and employment-related stress they had no time to sit and negotiate as to who would do what in their household. When the tasks needed to be done the important thing was to get them done without setting a score on who did what and how much.

Some husbands and wives under this model had traditional and opposing perceptions of each other's roles. While the husbands perceived themselves as heads of the household the wives wished to keep their control over household management in addition to their financial independence. Because they perceived themselves and their partners within the traditional role-relationship they were not prepared to bend the ground rules.

In their 21 years of marriage Mr. and Mrs. White had neither openly discussed their 'breadwinner' role nor they had any preconceived ideas of who should take the 'provider' role. When asked how he felt about his wife's paid work, Mr. White saw his wife's job as a 'fun doing' because she had fitted her paid work around the needs of their family. His interpretation of fun doing meant that she engaged in the labour force not so much because of economic reasons but to keep herself 'busy'. In this way she was a 'contributor' who added to the family income in addition to her home-making responsibilities. She also described her earning role as 'secondary' to her husband's main provider role.

126

Mrs. White: Well it is more appropriate for me to give up (paid work) because I am making less money. It comes down to economics and my job would be easier to quit.

When asked how they decided about their household roles she explained she just took on home-making responsibilities naturally.

Mrs. White: It still boils down to the woman doing more. I think in our household we both do a fair bit but being a woman I tend to think about it more. I mean I can't stand the mess...I mean I can't stand the lower level of mess that Ray (husband) can. Like if the clothes are not washed and ironed and so on...he wouldn't ever notice those sorts of things, whereas I would.

Not being able to stand a 'lower level' of mess meant Mrs. White felt guilty if the household work and family needs were either not met or not met properly. On the other hand Mr. White did not care about housework standards and said: 'She worries too much about it'. When asked how they felt about their family responsibilities they differed in terms of commitment and obligation.

Mrs. White: No I have no idea...I have thought about it before...but I don't really know why that is...(directs at husband) you know what I am talking about, why you can stand a higher degree of mess.
Mr. White: Well I don't think about it so I can't answer that.
Mrs. White: No, whether it's because you don't feel it's your responsibility and it doesn't worry you or whether you are preoccupied with your work...I don't know...deep in my soul I still think of the house as my responsibility.

Mr. White's job was considered a prime source of income, and therefore it largely excluded him from household responsibilities. When asked if he would clean the bathroom he indicated the boundaries.

Mr. White: (Laughs)...to a degree.
Mrs. White: (Nods)...no.
Mr. White: I mean to a certain degree...I mean I don't clean the bathroom...I...ah...I think you tend to look at priorities...which work is more important and worth doing.

While discussing their family roles the Turners talked about the current recession and the high cost of living. They had started their marriage with two incomes and did not discuss whether Mrs. Turner would continue her job as both their children were grown up. It was understood that she will continue to earn money for two reasons. First, there was economic necessity, Mr. Turner said: 'Today you can't have one person providing for the rest of the family. The cost of living is too high.' Second, Mrs. Turner was determined to maintain her financial independence.

> Mrs. Turner: Women who are financially independent are confident...like I don't have to ask for money...independent to spend on what and whom I like...but for a lot of years I couldn't ask for money because I wasn't earning and now I feel better.

Knowing how she felt about wanting to retain her independence and recognising economic necessity, Mr. Turner did not disagree with her decision. In other words, unlike the Hopes they had no qualms about who should or should not take upon the breadwinner role. However, they did disagree about their household division of labour. They were still 'battling' over task allocation. When asked who should be responsible for household work their response pointed to an unresolved conflict over renegotiation of the ground rules.

> Mr. Turner: It's not who is responsible but who gets more pressure put on them...if I walk across here and see the floor filthy I would do it.
> Mrs. Turner: I haven't seen him pick up the vacuum cleaner or clean up until I ask him.
> Mr. Turner: I picked up the vacuum cleaner yesterday.
> Mrs. Turner: That's true...that's because I was having a nervous breakdown and you were asked to, and with a lot of objection. He comes home and complains he is tired.

Mr. Turner does not initiate chore performance because he fears it would become his responsibility. He also feels that he should not do chores traditionally performed by women. Feeling overworked and frustrated, Mrs. Turner engages in overt negotiations to motivate her husband. When asked how they allocate household tasks they were quite open about it.

> Mr. Turner: She (wife) should do the housework and if she can't and I

128

have to then I would do it.

Mrs. Turner: I will be able to do a lot of things...strength wise...I don't have qualms about doing dirty jobs...but if it requires strength like wood chopping, chimney cleaning or mechanical I can't do it.

Mr. Turner did not mind sharing his provider role with his wife, but was not prepared to redefine the basic rules that governed their relationship as far as the household work was concerned.

'The man should be the main breadwinner' The Fields had begun their married life within a traditional pattern. However, due to economic necessity and a desire to pursue a career, Mrs. Fields went back to paid work after their third child. Now that they were in full-time jobs and raising three children under 16 they recalled the way events had taken shape over the past ten years.

Mrs. Fields: It's sort of like this, the way we were brought up we tend to think unconsciously that the father provide for the family and mother should do all of the housework and look after the children.

Mr. Fields: That would be nice but the necessity doesn't allow that...but if women want to go out they should be free to go out...they should have that choice. In our case economic necessity...declining life style...kids got older, ate more and need more clothes...living standard dropped.

Mrs. Fields: I sort of went back to work because a friend said to me why don't you...so I applied for a job...but when I got there Gurjeet...I just loved it being out amongst people again and realised how much I have been missing out on being at home.

For Mrs Fields the rewards doubled once she went back to paid work after child-bearing. Unlike the Whites, the Fields needed two incomes and Mr. Fields was much more willing to help in the household. However, if Mrs. Fields had her own way or if it was possible she would not take her husband's help in household work. She only took his help in absolute necessity.

Mrs. Field: It took us quite a while to work things out after I went back to work. If Jerry had to do the vacuuming or something I used to feel really angry and think I should be able to do that...but now because I have been back at work for quite a few years I don't react when he has to do things...we just do it very naturally...I don't feel guilty...whereas then I sort of felt that he'd feel not how he should feel if he had to do women's work.

In the process of renegotiating their household roles she went through a great deal of emotional torment. Being pragmatic, Mr. Fields was against his wife's desire to have a beautiful garden and a spotless house, because they were hard pressed for time. On the other hand, Mrs. Fields felt they should be able to have a good-looking front garden and a tidier home because she felt bad if people made a negative comment about the way they kept their household. When asked if they could give an example of a task that they were currently negotiating, they revealed what goes on behind the scenes.

> Mrs. Fields: It is the garden...isn't it Jerry? That is the only thing we ever have disagreement about.
> Mr. Fields: You want the garden and you want me to dig it...I'd say if you want the garden you dig it.
> Mrs. Fields: I have got a dream about...you know how you do...about a lovely garden?...But it involves Jerry doing a lot of hard work.
> Mr. Fields: It will involve me being a full-time gardener...that's not possible.

When asked who gets their way, they revealed Mr. Fields eventually digs the garden. Mrs. Fields said: 'I would keep on reminding him all the time and he does it to keep the peace don't you?' Mr. Fields nodded: 'yeah'.

The Browns did not consider the provider role as any one's particular responsibility. However, the rude awakening occurred when they encountered an incident at the local bank which made them rethink their egalitarian ideology about the breadwinner.

> Mrs. Brown: Who so ever can, should be the breadwinner...it doesn't have to be a single person.
> Mr. Brown: I think the male.
> Mrs. Brown: I think both depending upon the people involved in it and the arrangement.
> Mr. Brown: They don't do at the bank do they?
> Mrs. Brown: When?
> Mr. Brown: Automatically once they found out you (wife) had the higher income...that's why I didn't have the loan and then take that personally

from the loan or whatever...Leonie had the higher income and the bank manager just stopped talking to me and dealt with Leonie. That's the first time I ever felt the man should be the breadwinner.

Although the bank manager's way of dealing with the client was a normal procedure and one that had been in practice for many years, Mr. Brown's self image was questioned in the process. His breadwinning capacity was judged when the manager assessed his earning capacity to be lower than that of his wife. Mrs. Brown's income was found to be somewhat out of the ordinary by their immediate family members as well. She gave an example of her mother-in-law: 'John's mum is devastated that my earning capacity is more than John's...and she says women are not supposed to earn more than their husbands, she finds that very hard.'

In the past it had made sense, if Mrs. Brown continued to earn while her husband cut down his paid work to part-time so that he could take care of the baby and the home-making responsibilities. She said: 'John did very well, actually he should be working part-time and I should be working full-time once I get a little mobile when I am not breast feeding.' Mrs. Brown thought other people's reaction to their role-relationship was awful. She told her husband: 'I think some of your friends think I am an old dragon lady.'

Even though they had such liberal views about the breadwinner role they both agreed that the home-making responsibility was actually a 'woman's job'. This partially reflected Mrs. Brown's guilt at not being able to do things as and how she wanted them done.

Mr. Brown: I don't nag you.
Mrs. Brown: I would nag you. And sometimes you try to help me and you annoy me and I hate that. Just when I know where I am up to and you think you are helping me. I tell you (makes a face) back off and do your own thing, for example, when you try to help me with the washing I get angry and say back off I don't like the way you peg it anyway.
Mr. Brown: I usually give in to keep peace.

This agitated her and she often took it out on her husband. This occasional outburst does not depict a breakdown in their partnership but is an indication of their commitment to work things out.

In the Wills family the breadwinner role was still a sore point because it robbed Mr. Wills of his sole provider privileges. He felt the household roles should be arranged in such a way that the male should be the breadwinner and the female should stay home as there is enough to keep her occupied. Their conflict was still fresh after four years.

Mrs. Wills: I used to think it was right for a man...for all those years...to...to earn the living...but now...well.

Mr. Wills: I always thought it was wife's place to provide for everything (laughs)

Mrs. Wills: Well, I prefer to be a man myself...so what about you?

At the time Mr. Wills was the breadwinner he was unable to earn an adequate income for the family. Now that Mr. Wills was in the business mainly run by his wife he had to rely on her to guide him for certain decisions. Because of a lack of control over the family business he has taken the back seat as far as the household work was concerned.

In the early years of their marriage their household roles were gender-based. Renegotiation of chores in their household would require Mr. Wills to do a share of the household work which he was not prepared for. When they talked about their household roles prior to starting the business I had the feeling that Mrs. Wills was an enthusiastic worker. There was a certain 'sting' in their conversation.

Mr. Wills: I can't remember who did what...

Mrs. Wills: I can...

Mr. Wills: Tina did it all...

Mrs. Wills: I did it all...I did everything...we were renovating houses...and I will do everything else and I will turn up renovating houses as well...

Mr. Wills: So she is the heroine...

Mrs. Wills: Rubbish.

Their unsuccessful negotiation resulted from his lack of coming to terms with his wife's skills in operating the business. Now that she was a very successful business woman his attitude was non-co-operative. He found he was losing control over certain important family decisions. They gave an example.

Mrs. Wills: A decision about our daughter going overseas wasn't one which we sat down and talked about...Greg didn't want her to go away so I made the decision with her prodding and she went.

Mr. Wills: And I was the subservient male who finally said yes. That

132

wasn't in any way a democratic decision.

Keeping in mind his lost status he tried to retain the only power he had: his unwillingness to help in household work. Mrs. Wills decided to pay someone to do the household work to reduce conflict and avoid the negotiation of household work that had become a tedious task requiring a lot of time and energy.

The Fergusons had been together for nearly 10 years and had a gender-based division of labour. Mr. Ferguson felt that in any marriage the husband should be able to meet the family's economic needs so that the wife could have the choice of staying home. He was aware of his insufficient income and felt guilty: 'I should be able to provide for my family without my wife having to work so that she could have a choice.' Mrs. Ferguson also sympathised with many other families in which the wife had to be in paid work against her desire: 'In most cases women don't have a choice because they need to supplement income.'

They felt that marriage was a partnership between husband and wife in which 'give and take' was necessary to continue family life. Their household roles were based on a partnership derived from gender. They felt that if the wife earns an income the household work should be shared to reduce the burden. Strongly influenced by his parents' role relationship Mr. Ferguson said: 'You do things together and you are getting that help. That's how it worked with my mum and dad.' Their division of labour was shaped by gender and their likes and dislikes of chores. This pattern had emerged over the early years of their marriage.

Mrs. Ferguson: Ricky hates ironing.

Mr. Ferguson: I used to iron all the time when we first got married and she said: 'It's not a man's job', and I said: 'I won't do it and you will regret it', and I didn't do it and now she regrets it.

Mrs. Ferguson: No not really.

Mr. Ferguson: Anita works Monday to Friday and I will vacuum the house and dust the house and do the bathroom so that's done. My father did it so why shouldn't I do it. So it wasn't something that we sat down and said: 'Well you do this and I do that'. It happened.

Mrs. Ferguson: It just happened. So now we rarely highlight, each knows what to do.

Mr. Ferguson wished to involve himself in the household as he said: 'I'd love to be a house-father. I think I can cope quite well.' But Mrs.

Ferguson disliked his intervention and pushed him towards the masculine chores such as maintaining the yard, washing the family car and so on. This caused a considerable disagreement between them; however, Mrs. Ferguson was not yet prepared to give up her authority over household matters.

The Davidsons felt they had cruised through the years just as the society had wanted. They alluded to the fact that there are certain structural factors that help to shape couple's household roles. Mr. Davidson said: 'Well theoretically it shouldn't matter...but in our society husband is the main provider.' Over the last 17 years they had established gender-based roles.

> Mrs. Davidson: One of the reasons is that the continuity of the employment that if a woman discontinues employment then she often misses out on the advanced education and training whereas a man doesn't have the problem of having to go on maternity leave. It is easier for a man to be the main provider because the system just allows for that.

In their earlier years of marriage when they had no children they were both providers and they shared the household work equally. Mr Davidson said: 'It was almost equal sharing, we even went shopping together.' Soon after they had their first child Mrs. Davidson stopped working and the household work became more demanding and her sole responsibility. Without planning or discussing they fell into the traditional roles after having their children.

'It is not up to the woman to go out to work' Although Mr. and Mrs. Hope were both in full-time employment, becoming co-providers was not an easy task. Mr. Hope earned less than his wife, but he was not eager to give up his breadwinner role. When asked who the head of the household was in their family Mr. Hope said: 'It's me I suppose, I should provide I think.' He justified his status by relating to the way they were brought up. He further argued: 'I believe I am the boss and I am the provider in the family and my wife could have stayed at home if she wanted to but she likes to work and it's all right.' If he had his way he would not have allowed his wife to participate in the labour force. Knowing how her husband felt about her employment Mrs. Hope maintained her financial independence by accepting and struggling to meet her home-making responsibilities. When asked why she decided to go back to paid work after her children were born she told her short

history of child-bearing and child-rearing years.

Mrs. Hope: I worked up until my first child was born...then I had other children...you see I had four children in five years. We lost the second child. Then I started working when the youngest was 10 months. I had worked part-time just to get away from everything.

She had gone back to paid work without the consent of her husband. Knowing her husband's traditional attitude she did not make any attempt to renegotiate the ground rules of their family roles. Even then he felt the need to confirm his provider role by expressing his opinion on any marital role-relationship.

Mr. Hope: It is not up to the woman to go out to work...for her (wife) to work wasn't my opinion, that's for sure...I didn't want her to work even if she wanted to.

Knowing her husband was not prepared to relinquish his provider role Mrs. Hope declared: 'Yes, that's the way I look at things...and yes I am happy with that.'

Their household division of labour was based along traditional lines. Mrs. Hope said she enjoyed being a wife and a mother and liked to make sure that the household was run exactly the way she desired. In their early years of marriage Mrs. Hope was mainly responsible for housekeeping and regularly took her husband's help. This pattern continued through their early child-bearing years, especially when their babies were very young: 'He used to help me, he was a saviour and I couldn't have done without him.' In their family they never sat down to discuss who would do what around the house. As the children grew older they fell into the traditional pattern of 'man outdoor' and 'woman indoor' of doing things.

By choice Mr. and Mrs. Kerrington's household division of labour was negotiated along traditional lines. Mrs. Kerrington said: 'It is the wife's role to keep the house and if the husband is the main breadwinner she should do most of the household work.' She herself enjoyed being at home but disliked the household work. Mr. Kerrington admitted that since he had been married he had lost most of the housekeeping skills: 'I enjoy cooking. Most males lose that ability to do everything once you move from a bachelor to being a happily married man.'

135

'He often doesn't know what is for dinner' Mr. Turnbull agreed that more husbands than wives feel a little ashamed if they are not the main income earners. Rejecting the traditional notion of the male being the provider he said: 'It doesn't really matter if the woman is the main income earner...so it is up to the individuals to work out as a family unit.'

Similarly Mrs. Turnbull felt the times have changed: 'These days women are often just transferring their place of living to their own homes or their de-facto's or husband's home and take the job with them.' She felt in contemporary times the question is not who can provide but who can provide better, and who has the right qualifications or who can get a job. In their case they knew that both will continue to provide for the family and therefore did not engage in any negotiation about the main breadwinner role.

> Mrs. Turnbull: With respect to our household...we don't see it as totally my responsibility...in certain areas it might be my responsibility if you like...but Phillip (husband) lives here too...he has a say how the house is run.
>
> Mr. Turnbull: Jana probably does more of the organisation (looks at wife) you might organise the making of the curtains and the buying and that sort of thing...and I like to have a say what curtains we end up with...because I have other things too...Jana has her areas...but we both like to have a say in what is going on.

They had a gender-based household division of labour, where Mrs. Turnbull was responsible for the indoor chores and her husband for the outdoor chores. Mrs. Turnbull said: 'We don't actually sit down and divide it and say this is your area go and do it.' Their negotiation was unspoken and each was aware of the 'jobs' that needed doing. Overall they both took the responsibility for cleaning and maintenance jobs, but 'worrying' about the meals fell on Mrs Turnbull. Coming home from paid work required 'on the spot' negotiations on her part.

> Mrs. Turnbull: We might say coming home do you want to do the outside chores or do you want me to get the dinner going once we get there. But he (husband) often doesn't think what's for dinner and if I haven't got something already planned and when we get home there is nothing ready for dinner because he doesn't think that we go and eat at night.

136

Even though Mr. Turnbull did not take the initiative of planning and preparing the meals or doing any other indoor chores he wanted a clean and tidy household, especially the kitchen. Unlike other women respondents Mrs. Turnbull said: 'The times are gone when you just have to worry about the housework. It is something that is there, and there are more important things like play with son or talk to Phillip (husband) or go to work on time.'

Mr. Turnbull was often bothered and angry to see the place messy. He disliked his wife's lack of interest in keeping the house in order. Many times he took it upon himself to tidy up the household mess. This itself was a source of conflict.

> Mr. Turnbull: I tend to like to keep the place a little bit tidy. I get a little bit agitated when Jana...especially the kitchen...I hate to see the dirty dishes scattered everywhere...if I am cooking or whenever I am at home I'll clean up a little bit or leave them in the dishwasher or stack it so it looks fairly respectable whereas Jana just uses them and shoves them aside.

Seeing the house untidy on his arrival he underestimated his wife's input. Their conflict often resulted from the kitchen sink, which Mrs. Turnbull never perceived the same way as her husband did. Mrs. Turnbull stood her ground and said her husband underestimated the amount of household work she did before he arrived.

> Mr. Turnbull: I guess it even gets worse if I come and I had started early and had been to Tech. college and all the rest of it and come home and there is stuff all over the place...and Jana is watching Country Practice...(both laugh)...you know if I am working flat out why can't she just...
>
> Mrs. Turnbull: But you know what I do when I get home.
>
> Mr. Turnbull: I don't want to know...(mocks)
>
> Mrs. Turnbull: I give you three goes...when I get home I do the washing up, feed the animals, and I get the dinner going and probably make two or three phone calls and put Simon (son) to bed and then I might sit down.
>
> Mr. Turnbull: But then you sit down.
>
> Mrs. Turnbull: The moment you sit down your husband walks in...and 'oh you are sitting with your feet up'...I dislike the washing up too.

They had not yet come to an agreement about the messy kitchen which had become a 'sore point'.

Conclusions

I have analysed the couples' household work negotiation patterns and their family division of labour in Trade-off families and Rigid families. Couples under both models felt the provider role could be shared between the partners. However, during their child-bearing and child-rearing years it was practical to negotiate it on the basis of gender. This type of arrangement was considered favourable because of breast feeding, role suitability, preference, job structure and time availability.

The families under both models illustrated different patterns of role-relationships, especially by the ways in which they managed their households. Couples in families under the Rigid model had traditional and strict views about their household and marital roles. They also overtly and temporarily allocated chores under pressure. In contrast, due to their deliberate reorganisation of family life, the couples under the Trade-off model negotiated household division of labour more subtly, covertly and without distress. They also held more flexible views about household roles and ways of doing the household work. In other words, comparing families under Trade-off and Rigid models I found that the method of negotiation of household work and organisation of households was easier and less problematic in the former than latter.

There were three main reasons for such a difference. One was the husband's attitude towards household tasks in terms of what constitutes 'woman's job' and 'man's job'. Many husbands under the Rigid model did not clean the bathroom or toilet and were less willing to do so in future. Similarly they did not volunteer to perform the so-called 'woman's job' unless pressured by their wives. A task allocation was initiated by their wives to which they responded as 'helpers'. In contrast, in some families under the Trade-off model, if the wife was involved in full-time employment then the husband willingly initiated and participated in child-care and household chores that are traditionally performed by women.

A second aspect that contributed towards the difference between the two models was whether the families had renegotiated their tasks in line with life stage demands, time availability, and career interests. It appeared that families under the Trade-off model had renegotiated their

138

responsibilities and roles, whereas families under the Rigid model mainly left it to the wife to manage the household in addition to her paid work.

A third aspect that affected couples' wider role-relationship was the way they constructed their reality. Their outlook on life made a difference to the way they set out and met their ends. For example, couples under the Trade-off model lowered household work standards if they felt these were too difficult to realise. Similarly, some couples perceived chores objectively and no longer felt the need to define their identity through household work standards. These aspects of couples' role-relationship will be discussed in detail in Chapters 8 and 9.

Much of the difference in the ways in which couples under the two models handled their three-job situation depended upon the nature of household management rule 7 in Figure 3.3. Husbands and wives in families under the Trade-off model had flexible perceptions of their own and their partner's roles and of the household ground rules, and therefore they were able to negotiate tasks without conflict. In contrast, families under the Rigid model had conventional perceptions of their own and their partner's gender roles and the household ground rules, and therefore ran their households under conflict. Tables 7.1 and 7.2 confirm this, as the negotiation pattern under the Trade-off model indicates a fluid and flexible attitude towards household tasks. In contrast, couples in families under the Rigid model operated within a conventional way and therefore lacked a mutual approach to household work (see Tables 7.1 and 7.2). Similarly, partners' attitudes towards other's roles showed more positive, consensual and supportive judgement in Trade-off families and more negative and critical in Rigid families. This is shown in the distribution of (+) and (-) signs under 'Partner's Roles' in Tables 7.1 and 7.2.

8 Effective Management Versus Household Crisis

As seen in previous chapters, families under the Trade-off Model followed a specific set of household management rules (Figure 3.3) to deal effectively with household work contradictions. In contrast, families under the Rigid model were struggling to cope with household work contradictions, because they operated within traditional role ideology. Effective management of household work requires a specific arrangement of the household that fits in with the available resources of a three-job family. For example, if the couple is hard pressed for time and energy then they need to compromise on certain aspects of household work, such as a spotlessly clean and tidy home or a beautiful garden. It can then be claimed that in order to manage their households effectively, the couples need to redefine family order so it is suitable to their three-job situation.

In this chapter I extend the argument presented in the earlier chapters to rule 8, and detect whether the couples had redefined their family order to suit their three-job situation or not. I do this by analysing three aspects of the couples' relationships: 1) definition of family order; 2) quality of interaction; and 3) household management style. Specifically, it can be claimed that if a three-job family creates a hassle-free family order then they manage household work contradictions effectively.

In this book, 'family order' is defined as the 'organisation of family life in a specific manner.' Perception of family order varies between and within families. It is apparent from Table 8.1 that families under the Trade-off model created a flexible and negotiable family order in which they were prepared to try different ways to suit their three-job situation. In contrast, families under the Rigid model attempted to preserve themselves in conventional ways and wished to pursue a perfect home life. Similarly from Table 8.1 it can be observed that couples in Trade-off families engage in an interaction that is fairly unconventional and flexible, which led to a better management style. In contrast, couples' quality of interaction in Rigid families depicted disagreement, conflict and hostility. Their management style showed a lack of control over the situation.

Table 8.1 Redefinition of Family Order, Quality of Interaction and Household Management Style

Family Model (No)	Family Name	Redefinition of Family Order	Quality of Interaction	Management Style
Trade-off (20)	Burton	- We try to have a minimum social life (H) -With both working full-time, active social life is impossible so we deliberately avoid it (W)	-We have reversed roles in the past -Share housework through task specialisation -Discuss problems	-We handle things through priority
	Knight	-She works part-time because of small children (H)	-We step into each other's roles easily -The more you live with them the more you read them	-In crisis (car accident) situations -we have certainly pulled together
	Giles	-We have reorganised to have time for ourselves and the children (W) -I fit a lot more in these days (W)	-No need to negotiate they have hired help	-We worked hard in the past but now we enjoy the fruits of labour
	Simmons	-We plan ahead (H) -We are very well organised (W)	-They have a strict routine and share everything	-We don't go from crisis to crisis -We share the housework fifty fifty
	Stone	-With two full-time jobs it (life) was very difficult and we have avoided it (H)	-She is home early to do things	-She works part-time to manage things properly
	Broom	-We don't have a	-We have lived in	-We sort of work

	routine as it creates more problems and it gets worse (H) -We do things on a need's basis (H)	a communal household and the housework was a shared arrangement rather than as a couple	around it
Faldo	-We have a fairly unconventional tea time	-We probably read each other very well	-We complement each other
Long	-We have a chore list (W)	-Reminds him to the point of nagging	-We seem to deal with daily crisis just fine
Jenning	-Order is pretty stupid (H) -We compromise and re-establish order (W)	-He is beginning to see things her way	-We are not good at crisis management
Fielding	-I love to come to a clean house and mess puts pressure on me (W)	-She calls her mother to help her husband	-Mum helps so it is OK
Simpson	-This household operates at a consistent rate (H)	-He helps her during the working term	-We just go with the flow
Sands	-When it becomes too difficult we just leave it until another day (H)	-We remind each other subtly and sometimes not so subtly	-We manage fairly well
Drummond	-We don't have a routine (W)	-Husband takes the baby away when things become too much, negotiation is not considered necessary	-I only find crisis when he (Husband) is here
Harris	-I don't feel comfortable if the house has got to a unbearable stage	-He has left the responsibility for finding the baby sitter on her	
Donovan	-I am not fussy (H) -Kids are very easy and used to my habits (W)	-He understands the 'are you hungry' question	
James	-I am not a very good home maker (W)	-They involve children to help in the household	

142

Rigid (14)	Richards	-I feel regimented about cleaning the house (W)	-I have learned not to nag but compromise his way of doing chores otherwise he will say do it yourself	-There are pressures we are not denying that
	Short	-We have a certain amount of mess all the time (W)	-I have to ask him and beg the kids to help	-I get frustrated because I don't know how to involve children
	Mason	-In a crisis situation I will stay up late and finish the housework	-He doesn't mind the mess	-I'd rather stay cranky and get it done
	Black	-Children take priority but the housework is at the back of my mind	-She asks him and he helps her	-We manage by not doing many tasks
	Ferguson	-Feeding the children is important (W) -Mainly worry about the children (H)	-Each knows what to do	
	Kerrington	-I think it is wife's role to keep the house (W)	-she gets angry and asks every one to come and help	-When they come and help things are normal again
	Davidson	-If the house is a mess we have a white tornado (W)	-She rounds up everyone to do the housework	-If it is a negotiated chore she will just nag until it is done
	White	-People are amazed that I can do what I do and still the house looks clean and I think the house doesn't look very clean (W)	-She starts yelling and shouting	-With women working the families probably live in a muddle and have lower standards
	Fields	-I have got a dream about a beautiful garden (W)	-They disagree over standards -She keeps asking husband for help	-We cope by accepting that we can't cope -We would say don't come and visit us it is terrible and we would be embarrassed
	Hope	-I like to make sure the house is clean and everything is done properly (W)	-When tension builds she throws temper tantrums	-We have brought up our children to help around the house

143

Turner	-It is nice if people come and the place is tidy (W)	-They make each other guilty she pressures husband to help by yelling and shouting then she has a nervous breakdown	-When the going gets tough the tough (wife) gets going
Turnbull	-I hate to see the dirty dishes scattered every where (H) -Housework is not something I live for (W)	-She gets angry and jumps up and down, and arguments begin	
Brown	-If the place is not clean you get agitated about little things (W)	-She nags him and he gives in to keep peace -She blows up every now and then yells at him	-We cope by neglecting the housework -She blows up every now and then yells at him
Wills	-Everyone has to be fed first (W)	-She confronts him and gives orders	-She confronts him and gives orders

Trade-off families

Families under the Trade-off model differed in their household management style from families under the Rigid model, mainly in the ways in which they had reorganised their family in line with available resources. They had redefined their perceptions of what constituted a good family life. Through trial and error they had also learned that a renegotiated family arrangement can be practicable and satisfying.

Mr. and Mrs. Burton were both in full-time employment and had a daughter under two years who was not yet settled with her baby sitter. They found this very traumatic, both for them and their daughter. They felt the need to restructure their life style so that they could spend more time with her. The intensity of crisis could not be minimised by becoming a one-income family because they needed two incomes to pay off mortgage on their family home. At the time of interview they expressed their dilemmas of paid work versus family needs. They had also cut down on their social life so that they could allocate any spare time to family activities especially with their daughter.

144

'It is just a matter of reorganising'   Mr. Burton: Our daughter comes first. We have reorganised around her.

> Mrs. Burton: We sort of try and have a minimum social life. Because if we are both working full-time and trying to combine that active social life as well, it is next to impossible. Because if you are having people over for dinner or anything, first you have to clean up the place to make it presentable, and after they are gone you have to clear the mess. So we deliberately avoid it.

In situations where the wife was employed part-time and the couple engaged in an egalitarian division of labour, they experienced very few hardships. They valued time as a scarce but essential resource, especially if the children were at their earlier stages of development. Young children constantly required parental guidance that was not always possible when the parents were hard pressed for time and energy. Mr. and Mrs. Knight felt strongly about their involvement in their children's development. By organising her paid work hours to a manageable load Mrs. Burton enjoyed her part-time teaching job and family life. In their family they did not face household work crisis. They defined crisis as something external to household work and beyond control.

> Mrs. Knight: In a crisis we have certainly pulled together. A perfect situation was last Friday when I had an accident in my car so I was a bit shaken from that.

In the beginning the Giles faced numerous hardships due to a lack of time, money and energy. They worked continuously for three years without a holiday to set up the business. They said this was the most trying time for them. Mrs. Giles recalled the hardships.

> Mrs. Giles: I find I don't have those situations now but we used to have them. Danny will come home and I will go off my head, go into the bedroom, and say I can't cope, it is all too much. So the way we have organised now we can have the time for ourselves and the children. I find I fit a lot more in the day what I did before.
> Mr. Giles: Yes, it's just a matter of organisation.

145

They reduced their time spent in monotonous household chores through hired help. They paid someone to mow the grass and clean their house so that they could enjoy pleasant tasks such as gardening.

The Simmons faced housework crises infrequently, because they had co-ordinated their household in a particular way. They had adopted a strictly organised system which they did not wish to change. They were both employed full-time and had three school age children. They always planned ahead, their shopping was always done, their meals were prepared in advance and they just followed the routine. They explained the secret of effective management in the following manner.

> Mr. Simmons: No, we don't go from a crisis to crisis. I like to plan things so we know exactly what we are doing.
> Mrs. Simmons: We are very well organised. We don't plan meals at 5.30 and say what are we going to eat tonight. You can't do that with three children or you can have McDonald's every night.

Sometimes families were forced to reorganise themselves if they faced frequent and intense hardships as a result of wife's role overload. In the past the Stones had faced similar problems through having two full-time jobs and caring for two children. In addition, Mr. Stone's paid work involved shifts that upset their family routine. They confessed they had chaos in their household and consequently they were forced to cut down Mrs. Stone's paid work hours to accommodate the needs of everyone in the family.

Mr. and Mrs. Stone believed that a reorganisation of their priorities was an expression of being responsible parents. When asked if they could relate to specific hardships they responded by comparing their present situation with the times when Mrs. Stone was involved in full-time employment. They said they had always been in a rush to get things done and lacked control. Now that Mrs. Stone was employed part-time and was home to prepare the meals they faced fewer hardships. Because their meals were organised they could avoid a number of problems. Although they had only two children they had to prepare different dishes to suit their individual tastes. Cooking different things for different members took much organisation and preparation but it also showed their commitment as parents. After facing serious hardships because of two full-time jobs they had found a schedule that suited their family.

Mr. Stone: It was lot harder when Ann worked full-time. When you are working full-time and you are always in a rush it is a very different situation. We have avoided this because you are very tired and it is much easier to be part-time.

Mrs. Stone: I did have that situation when I worked full-time. Oh, it was terrible.

They found they faced fewer hardships with this manageable load. They were also able to do a number of family-related activities such as going for bike rides and playing with children.

Through years of experience, Mr. and Mrs. Long had reorganised their household division of labour to minimise the household work burden on one person. Their teenage children were given chores which they performed without fuss. However, they faced problems when Mr. Long had to leave town on employment-related trips. In addition, because they worked hard and were over-tired and stressed they were unable to do other things that normal families did. For example, going on camping and pursuing recreational activities were out of the question. Mrs. Long recalled occasions when her husband had to be out of town on a business trip.

Mrs. Long: We seem to deal with daily crisis just fine because the way we revolve but I remember when Dave used to travel a lot I was under a lot of stress. I had to do everything.

Household work problems affected members of the family in different ways. One partner might ignore the rush to get things done whereas the other maybe distressed just by the thought of it. It was interesting to observe a variation in the meanings taken by husbands and wives of the same event.

'We do things on a needs basis'   The pressures that impinged on families were either external, or internal and as a result families' interpersonal relationships were affected. Mr. and Mrs. Broom avoided trivial pressures that caused unnecessary hardships for their family. They simply lowered their household work standards and avoided the hassles of meeting social demands for doing things in a specific way to please others. They deliberately avoided a routine and performed tasks on a needs basis. They also shared household work and parenting tasks,

and therefore no particular person had household work responsibility. This type of division of labour required a greater understanding and honesty on their part which they maintained very well. They had three children under twelve who were present at the time of interview. It was past nine pm and the children were not yet bathed or asked to change and prepare for bed. They were aware of their lower standards but did not feel embarrassed.

> Mr. Broom: Well, we are not very organised and we don't have much of a routine and do things on a needs basis as you can look around. Instead of saying you have to go to bed at seven or bath them at the same time each night we are fairly easy that way.

In fact they claimed that their adaptable routine was suitable to their life style, as they both worked in flexible jobs and had very few employment-related pressures. Mrs. Broom's paid work involved being on call at a short notice. The unpredictability of her job impinged on their household routine. They described their current life stage and Mrs. Broom's job situation as the main reasons being for their family disorganisation.

> Mr. Broom: My work is extremely flexible and Marian can be called to work at any time so it is silly for us to have a routine. That creates more problems and it gets worse. We have three little children and we are not living in a white shaggy pile carpet you know with plastered walls where you have to take care of it.

When children are young, parents face several hardships due to a lack of time, money and energy. When they grow up and become self-sufficient then parents look back and remember that life stage in nostalgia. The Faldos described how the years when they faced hardships had passed like a tornado. Because their children had moved to the life stage of young adulthood they were no longer directly responsible for their welfare. They were in their early forties and had been in paid work throughout their prime years. In this way they were in a comfortable financial situation. They recalled the life stage when they faced hardships of combining paid work and responsibilities rather nostalgically.

> Mrs. Faldo: Barney wasn't particularly happy with the job he was doing.

He will come home after dealing with small children all day and his own children were running to the door calling, daddy, daddy and he will try to talk to the children but his eyes were saying give me five minutes. I used to know he wanted to be alone.

Through hindsight the Faldos felt that parents should make the most of the time with their children. At the time of the interview they faced no serious hardships apart from an occasional stressful day.

Some families were working out different household routines to suit their particular family situation. Whereas some wives wished to hang on to the traditional ways of keeping the household, the others did not bother. Most husbands were not fussy and willingly adapted to new routines and unconventional ways of doing things.

Frustration and household work crisis

'I tend to get angry and yell' In the case of Mr. and Mrs. Jenning both differed in the way they perceived the household work contradictions and consequently reacted to problematic situations differently. They disagreed on certain household work issues, for example, they lacked a shared perspective on what degree of cleanliness constituted a clean house. Their conflict emerged through a chain reaction. For example, if Mrs Jenning was tired and unable to cope with a number of demands then she would get angry and lose control. Her bad mood interfered with a normal family interaction. She would get further distressed to the point where everyone would feel unhappy.

> Mr. Jenning: We are not very good at crisis management, the stress is the need to get things done quickly. Whether we haven't planned things or run out of time.
> Mrs. Jenning: I get stressed if I get too much work to get through. I get very angry and hysterical but Garry is even-tempered and nothing seem to rattle him.
> Mr. Jenning: I get stressed if you get stressed.

Paid work together with providing care for three children under five requires time and patience. Mrs. Fielding felt overworked and stressed and explained that keeping the place clean was problematic because she needed not only time but energy to do the work. As soon as she finished tidying up the house their three children messed it up. She described a

149

situation in which conflict resulted from her inability to maintain a tidy home.

> Mrs. Fielding: I tend to get angry and yell. I sort of blow-up and rage around the place and then nobody makes me cranky. I love to come to a clean house. If I come to a messy house it puts pressure on me.

Mrs. Harris experienced a difficult situation in her household when her son required her attention during evening meals. She said: 'Nothing could be worse than chasing around a toddler with a spoon trying to feed.' Putting up with her son's fuss over the food and having to perform household work at the same time caused a big commotion in the evenings. She said: 'I feel cranky with myself because I can't do things as quickly as I want them to be done.' Much of her anxiety was due to her inability to do things the way she had done in her childless years.

> Mr. Harris: You get bossy in those situations. Like, do this or do that.
> Mrs. Harris: Yes bossy, you know, I guess I am the sort of person who can't relax until it is done at the level I want.

She was used to a clean and tidy home because she was able to maintain a higher household work standards before her son was born. Even though she was employed only for a few hours a week she spent much of her time looking after her son and doing the household work. This frustrated her because there was always something that needed her attention.

'It is just full on and beaten' The need to prepare for the following day took much of Mr. and Mrs. Simpson's free time after they had finished the daily routine. They had hired help once a week to reduce the burden of some of the household work. However, they found themselves doing chores late at night to make the next day a smooth one. They felt the game had to be played and the children have to be given a normal childhood so they both combined their resources to do their best for the family.

> Mrs. Simpson: Between work and home it just becomes too busy but it's not 'jangling'. It is just full on and beaten, that's not something you can sit still and worry either, because you just got to keep going.

They found the early child-rearing stage a real hardship because of a lack of time, money and energy. In order to manage two paid and one unpaid job they had to postpone other goals until the children were old enough to care for themselves. The hardships in the Simpson household were perceived to be due to Mrs. Simpson's full-time teaching career which she could not negotiate to part-time. However, being a school teacher she found certain benefits in not having to worry about holiday and after-school child-care. Her school-related work (marking, preparing teaching material, report writing) kept her extremely busy through the week and especially during weekends. Consequently, paid work and family demands impinged on her own personal time for relaxation.

> Mr. Simpson: It's our real night off because you are here, otherwise we never sit like this. There are times when you feel a little dizzy and you are feeling crook in your stomach. The life is just going on. I'd just put the kids to bed and she will say might as well make some lunches and she will go and put a load of washing so it can be hung tomorrow. You see you never sit down.
> Mrs. Simpson: You never sit and relax because you will just get bogged.

Coupled with their life stage demands, another reason for chaos in the Simpson family was employment-related stress. A denial of stress was a strategy used by them in order to avoid the acceptance of a 'loss of control'. over their household. Despite stress symptoms every attempt was made not to 'give in' but 'keep going'. Mr. Simpson said: 'You say oh I feel dizzy in the head whereas normally you are completely relaxed. I don't put it down to stress, but it could be. I might say it could be that I have eaten something, could be the stomach nerve.'

Mrs. Donovan, a secretary, had the opportunity to be employed full-time and make more money; however, she felt her two children would suffer if they had to go to after-school child-care. She often found herself in a unbearable situation.

> Mrs. Donovan: Because I only have so much time and I like to achieve a lot so I can spend sometime with the children. Here the children are doing something or fighting and I am trying to complete this task. I found what I wanted to achieve wasn't achievable so I will grit my teeth and send them to their rooms.

151

'He's got the luxury of doing the crisis'   As mentioned earlier, one of
the reasons for conflict in three-job families was a change of wife's
status through employment. The decision to go back to paid work did
not always come through a choice, as it was because of economic
necessity. Women also worked for self development rather than being
housewives and mothers. Some women required time away from the
household because it became too much for them. Contributing to their
disappointment, in spite of their hard work, was the non-rewarding
nature of household work. When asked to describe the hardships, some
husbands showed a lack of awareness of the burdensome nature of
keeping a household.

> Mr. Sands: Well, Rene does most of the housework and she manages very
> well. She is so efficient, most of the things are done by the time I get
> around to do them, I never get to mow the lawn that's done.
> Mrs. Sands: Someone has to avoid the crisis.

The Drummonds had a 12-months-old daughter who could be very
persistent. During the times Mrs. Drummond worked their daughter was
with a baby sitter. After picking her up Mrs. Drummond did the daily
shopping, and by the time she got home a number of other chores
demanded her attention. Consequently she could never organise the
evening meals in advance to give quality time to their daughter. It was
during evening meal preparation they faced problems.

> Mrs. Drummond: In the evening I might be cooking something and she is
> going around demanding me and finally I might 'lose out' then.

Mrs. Drummond said she never saw the 'mess' when she was growing
up, and her mother always reminded her to clean up the mess properly:
'Before we had our daughter we didn't have to worry about the mess.'
Now Mrs. Drummond feels even her husband adds to the mess: 'I never
feel the crisis when I am on my own. I only find it a crisis when Rob
(husband) is here and he's got the luxury of doing the crisis.' What she
meant was that her husband did not take the responsibility like she did.

> Mrs. Drummond: I don't think men see it as women see it. You know what
> I mean, they can't see it, they are blind (both laugh). If you keep on
> picking up those crumbs from under the toaster it doesn't escalate,
> everything is maintained. If you don't it always reaches a 'crisis point'

and then you have a 'big clean-up'.

As a result of a lack of time and energy it became essential for some families to involve their children in household work in order to reduce hardships. This shows the pressures faced by couples in the process of managing employment and family responsibilities. By involving children and increasing the available personnel assets the hardships of household work were significantly reduced. The James family faced a crisis in household work but managed to cope with the help of their children. However, a difficult situation resulted during school holidays when Mrs. James could not take time off to care for her children. Mr. James could take time off during winter to stay with them but during summer his job demands did not permit him to take any time off. They related an incident when they had to leave the children on their own.

> Mrs. James: My family is not living here and we are not close to my husband's family and one time our son was sick and we both couldn't take time off. We face such crises many times.

Rigid families

Families under this model faced more problems than families under the Trade-off model because they were not prepared to compromise and renegotiate what constituted a 'good family life'. Although these families faced similar structural constraints as families under the Trade-off model, they differed in the way in which they constructed their 'family order'. They were living in a three-job family with fewer resources, but they wanted to have all the luxuries of family life.

Traditional family order

'I would like to see her home at a sensible hour and the dinner cooked' Sometimes a balance between paid work and family was disrupted by a sudden external or internal demand. For example, the family might have had a routine which was upset by some reason such as one parent having to stay back at their paid work, an empty fridge, or other unanticipated events that required immediate attention. Consequently, due to hunger, fatigue and a lack of planning, chaos

153

resulted during the evening meal. Such situations were described similar to a panic during black-out.

> Mr. Richards: One problem is that we both have careers, sometimes job demands are more than nine to five. I would like to see her (wife) home at a sensible hour and the dinner cooked before I arrive.
>
> Mrs. Richards: There are pressures in a both working situation and we are not denying that. You have to be highly organised, and if something upsets that organisation that's when the trouble starts.

Mrs. Richards' priorities were to maintain higher household work standards, whereas her husband differed with regard to what constituted cleanliness. Although he helped her in the household work by cleaning the bathroom he did it on a needs basis. He sometimes neglected it for too long and the issue became a source of conflict, not only because he did not perform this chore regularly but also he did not do it properly. Mrs. Richards had tried to renegotiate the rules as to how and when she liked the tasks to be done, but failed to convince her husband. On the other hand, Mr. Richards felt if he had the responsibility of a chore then he should be the one to decide when and how it should be done.

> Mrs. Richards: Andrew really knows bathrooms and toilets are his responsibility and he won't do them every Sunday morning.
>
> Mr. Richards: I do them on needs basis, my eyesight is not so good (jokes) and she tends to see the dirt first.
>
> Mrs. Richards: And sighting that I have learned not to nag about it, because his attitude to nagging is 'oh well do it yourself' and I 'keep my peace' and pretend I haven't noticed.

Mrs Short had joined the labour-force out of economic necessity. A sudden change in her role from a full-time mother and a wife to an employed mother and wife contributed to a series of chaotic situations in the family.

> Mrs. Short: When I started work I took Sam's time-table and said this is when his lectures are and I can work the other time and he will be home to look after the youngest son. This allowed us only half-an-hour to take over, and if his lectures went over then it just threw the whole bag, then we have to be home for the middle one to be off the bus and we were getting restless. It wasn't working. We need another car and more

money, then I wouldn't have to work on the week-ends and we could do more things as a family.

Mr. Short: She would withdraw.

Mrs Short: I withdraw, then Sam will get frustrated and then there will be a conflict.

Some of the hardships they faced were because of a sudden change in her status, a lack of second car and her doubled work overload that led to other changes in the household, such as the need to negotiate household roles and put up with lower household work standards. These caused a conflict in their marriage. Off and on they had a row over who did more around the house. At the time of interview washing the dishes was a point of concern because both felt that should be the other's responsibility. Mr. Short said: 'We don't really have an argument about who does more of the washing up but we have a feeling about it.' On the other hand Mrs. Short felt irked with the household work and contemplated taking more help from her children: 'I speak to the kids really nicely and ask for help but they go and play and forget about it, I just don't know how to do it without being a nagging old mother.'

'When you have small children it is difficult' Household work was considered a huge task, requiring skill, care, and often physical and mental endurance. If neglected it not only piles up, but can lead to a disagreement between the couple. To illustrate this point we will consider the Mason household. Mrs. Mason was employed full-time and therefore had limited time and energy to do the household work. Their children often left their dirty clothes and toys everywhere and the place became messy. As things often progressively got worse, she became distraught and told everyone off. On the other hand it did not bother her husband because he believed: 'There is always tomorrow'. His response further frustrated Mrs. Mason and consequently they had a disagreement and she ended up doing the household work until late at night.

Mr. Mason: A crisis is when we come home both tired and we are both cranky and there are things left from the morning that need to be done and the place is a mess for some reason. When you have small children it is difficult.

Mrs. Mason: I have got off to work and come back there are clothes every where. What do I do when I am stressed? Get super efficient at tidying

155

things.

Mrs. Mason knew if she had not straightened up the place the night before, the next day would not be an easy one. She also knew she would have to do it, and she therefore preferred to 'get it out of the way'.

Reaction to household work crisis

'I have a good yell and get it out of the system'   Mr. and Mrs. Black were raising three young children. They faced hardships mainly because of their life stage demands and a lack of resources. They coped with this life stage by postponing several tasks that were rationalised as non-essential, for example, the task of bed making and tidying up some parts of the household were deliberately ignored. Any situation that caused problems in child-care routine was taken seriously and tackled spontaneously.

> Mrs. Black: In a crisis situation there are a number of things demanding attention at the same time. Like the kids need to be bathed, dressed, fed, read to, and tucked-in. Then, the fire has to be started, the meal has to be prepared, the dog has to be fed and the next day's preparations the lot.
> Mr. Black: That is the source of stress actually.
> Mrs. Black: I have a good yell and get it out of the system. A big blow-up and that's it, it's gone. I think sometimes you get a bit cross and you yell and whatever.

Mrs. Black felt her entire time was spent in taking care of little things around the house and organising children's activities. She said: 'Sometimes you get yourself into so many things it's not worth it, I often feel exhausted.' Physical exhaustion led to other forms of behaviour, such as losing her temper and being verbal. She admitted having an occasional yell or a big blow up every now and then helped her relieve the tension. Some days she was unable to carry out even the essential chores because of physical tiredness. Mr. Black also felt deprived of personal time: 'If I had free time I would do absolutely nothing and sleep a bit more.'

Much of the debate in the Ferguson household was about task allocation and household work standards, particularly ideals of mothering and home-making. Like women who have their higher standards of household work, husbands have their own which their wives don't accept kindly. We will take an example from the Ferguson household that often led to conflict. Mr. Ferguson had been polishing the floor ever since they moved to their present family home. In order to maintain its shine he had to spend a lot of time and energy. On the other hand, through experience Mrs. Ferguson knew her husband's efforts were wasted because their three small children were too young to remember to take their shoes off as they often came running in. She found this monotonous chore was a waste of time and energy.

Mr. Ferguson: If I get frantic about the floor I would just go and do it. Anita (wife) will say you don't have to do it will get dirty again. Even if I know it is going to get dirty again I still have to do it and get yelled at. I do it just to make me feel good.

Mrs. Ferguson: I can probably highlight things he would rather be doing, for example, Ricky (husband) never washes the car.

Mr. Ferguson: I have washed the car.

Mrs. Ferguson: Yes, but only after reminding you two or three times.

The Kerringtons faced a different set of problems that required tolerance and careful decision-making. Decisions that involved their teenage children often led to their stress. The intensity of conflict was measured by the amount of stress experienced by both parents. Because there was a sudden change in their children's status on entering high school they had to redefine their parenting standards in order to respect their children's rights. Many times a lack of shared understanding between both parents on setting the boundaries for their children led to a conflict.

Mrs. Kerrington: It has happened where things are in a crisis. When you are uptight and have an argument and start yelling. Children stress me more than anything else. Making decisions for them you know, what should I do, should I send them to the party or not. I want to be fair. You have to be careful.

Mr. Kerrington: I tell Lucy it's up to them. They have to pass their exams, they have to take the responsibility for that not me. I can cajole, I can't do everything, they have to do it.

The Kerringtons were going through a stage when they had to renegotiate rules with their children. This was not an easy task, especially for Mr. Kerrington, who lacked skill and patience in interacting with his teenagers.

The Davidsons were fairly relaxed about household work and performed chores on needs basis. Since they were living just outside the town they did not receive many unexpected visitors. Mrs. Davidson said a panic would start in their family when they received a phone call about visitors arriving. At that moment they would realise their family home is not presentable to their guests. Mrs. Davidson said: 'I will start yelling and ask everyone to get their act together'. Being hospitable to their visitors was very important to them; they perceived this as making their home welcoming and comfortable. A sort of panic would set in when they are unable to clean up and prepare for their visitors on time.

Sometimes it took outsiders to remind a family about its inconsistencies and neglect of household work. At the announcement of a visitor the family would evaluate its physical environment to see if it was presentable or not. Would it make the visitor welcome? What kind of impression will their home set for the visitor? These questions were basic for providing hospitality. A well presented home was considered inviting, welcoming and hospitable.

Some families tried to adhere to a household arrangement in which things were done perfectly and conventionally. They believed that a good family life was one that had home-cooked nutritious meals, a clean and tidy home, a beautiful garden and things in a proper order. As the main responsibility of managing the household routine was on wives they continually faced problems.

'In crisis I would probably start yelling'   Mr and Mrs White experienced household problems that resulted from several contributing factors. These included their two full-time careers, a lack of money to buy adequate hired help, their three school age children's demands, and their involvement in a number of community activities. In addition, Mr. White's reluctance to relinquish some of his paid work-related commitments to come home on time and help his wife, and Mrs White's commitment to teaching music at their home in the evening, exacerbated the problems. Their competing priorities often led to a disruption in family routines.

> Mrs. White: Our crisis is mainly getting too busy, too many things happening too quickly, and we can't handle that. Things like that and

158

other commitments, our involvement in the local music around the town...it's not my work only but other things we are involved with or in charge of and get mixed up.

Mr. White: Yes, I think at times I find it difficult to cope with commitments.

In a crisis situation, Mrs. White would react overtly to tell everyone how she felt about their disorganised household. In most cases, the trouble started from a messy house. Being responsible for keeping the home 'tidy and beautiful' she would take charge and make no exception about telling others how she felt about it.

Mrs. White: I am usually more cranky with the kids probably. In crisis I would probably start yelling a lot wouldn't I ? (looks at Ray).
Mr. White: You worry too much.

Similarly, the Fields faced crises due to a lack of resources, the demands of their three school age children, two careers and their commitment to a number of other goals. Over the past few years Mrs. Fields had started to upgrade her qualifications. However, she also continued to prepare nutritious meals, and keep the house and garden spotlessly clean and tidy. They mentioned several incidents that could lead to household problems.

Mr. Fields: Before we had the children, Tracy did the lot, and we didn't make a mess. But now once they clean their teeth they leave it all over the hand basin, have a shower and leave all the soap everywhere.
Mrs. Fields: He says that because people make a mess, Jerry (husband) is tracking them down. In a crisis situation we would say it is terrible, don't anyone visit us because I'd be embarrassed. You see if I have got some study to do and children who need help with their homework, and my school work and things, it all can't be done, and I try to stay calm.

Because Mrs. Fields has deliberately and willingly taken on the main responsibility of home-making she accepts her limitations. However, she does not want her extended family and friends to find out what goes on 'back stage'.

While having two incomes provided the Fields with definite benefits, it took away a substantial amount of their time and energy. Time spent at paid work was generally time lost for family activities such as household work, child-care, leisure, and so on. Consequently, any time for essential family interaction and necessary household activities was perceived as a limited resource. Mr. and Mrs Fields described household work crisis to be a situation that resulted from excessive work demands, a lack of essential resources (time and energy) and their own inadequate responses to these demands. Often stress was the result of meeting higher household work standards. Frequently they left the household in a rush in the morning and found it messy and untidy. When they returned in the evening they felt inadequate and not in control.

'When I am angry I tend to jump up and down' Mrs. Hope started paid work at eight-thirty in the morning and finished around five pm. By the time she got home it was well after five-thirty. She relies on her husband to drop off and pick up their two children from school, and also to keep the household in a reasonably tidy condition. Problems began when Mrs. Hope returned from work tired and worn out, and found the house untidy. As an employed mother, she not only felt guilty but angry, for not being able to fulfil her responsibilities.

> Mrs. Hope: I like to make sure my house is clean because that's my first priority. But housework is like building a castle with blocks and someone knocks it down and you have to do it again and again.

Pressures of full-time employment, coupled with her husband's lack of support for her paid work, often led to her frustration. However, not wanting to make things worse for themselves she blamed herself for disruption in their household. She admitted she tried to compensate for her absence from the home by working even harder. This further added to her stress and fatigue. The following accounts depict a typical hectic day.

> Mr. Hope: We both have our own things to do around the house and when Ingrid has too much inside then I come and rescue her.
> Mrs. Hope: If I came home and I am cranky and the place isn't tidy then I throw a little tantrum and Dennis (husband) will calm me with a cup of coffee and we sit somewhere. When one feels the pressure the other will take over.

Throwing a tantrum meant Mrs. Hope was unable to cope with household work. This was a signal to her husband to help her with household work. Fatigue and stress were physical and psychological restrictions that her husband could not argue against. Mrs. Hope did not openly announce 'household crisis' because it was perceived to be a result of her absence from the household. She also knew she had chosen paid work against her husband's wishes, so therefore was determined to make things work.

A similar crisis was experienced by the Turners. When asked: 'Who should be responsible for household work?' Mr. Turner justified that it was his wife's role to keep the house. They outlined a conflict over their conception of task allocation and performance. The following accounts show how household work negotiations can be troublesome and sarcastic.

Mrs. Turner: We usually talk about it, don't we?
Mr. Turner: Yes, we talk about it and make the other people feel guilty.
Mrs. Turner: But we don't go yelling and screaming about it (Looks at husband). Do we go yelling and screaming?
Mr. Turner: Yes, we go yelling and screaming quite a few times...someone will turn around and say 'well it's your turn'.

Because Mr. Turner was reluctant to renegotiate the basic rules permanently, he helped now and then when pressured to do so. In this way he remained a helper and did not commit himself to household work

Trouble would begin in the Turnbull household as soon as they picked up their son at five pm. Mrs. Turnbull described the tiring nature of her multiple responsibilities: 'Well on the way home I am rehearsing what is there to eat? What needs to be done for tomorrow? Is there enough food in the fridge?' She said if she has a few minutes with her husband before they pick up their son she can plan ahead for the evening.

Mrs. Turnbull: I find if I am trying to talk to Phillip about something and our son is yelling in the back I get very wound up very quickly. I do get stressed very easily and when I am angry I tend to jump up and down. I am not good at hiding and pretend everything is all right. I tend to let it out and forget what I was yelling about five minutes later and everyone else is sitting there and shivering.
Mr. Turnbull: The thing that stresses me is just having to do so many things. This happens virtually every morning and every night.

Their employment-related costs such as substitute child-care, a second car and convenient food items did not allow them the luxury of hired help.

'Blast at the weekend wouldn't be for the first time' During their childless years the Browns had two high incomes and regularly used domestic help, but since they had had their two children they were hard pressed for essential resources. With their current expenditure they were unable to afford the much-needed house help. They confessed to not being disorganised when they had their first child, as a 2:1 parent child ratio worked very well. But when both were employed, many chores were performed hurriedly and therefore required attention again and again. Besides caring for two small children, they seemed to be doing everything around the house, except that they gave too little time to everything and consequently nothing was done properly. Repairs, general maintenance and spring cleaning never seemed to be taken care of.

> Mrs. Brown: In the beginning of the week it is okay but it's had it by Friday, because we work and tend to dump everything to survive. Whereas some major chores are completed under crisis circumstances because they have been totally neglected. I know when enough is enough which leads to frustration and I blast. I usually yell at you don't I?
> Mr. Brown: Blast at the weekend that's when we raise our voices and that wouldn't be for the first time.

Life stage demands and a lack of resources had led the Browns to neglect the household work and postpone chores until the end of the week, but eventually they had to face the neglected chores.

Sometimes one partner differed as to whether a situation was a crisis or not. They were also less likely to solve the problem. Under these circumstances they tried to convince the other partner to see it their way. Such disagreement became problematic and exacerbated the conflict. In the Wills' household Mr. and Mrs. Wills and their teenage children did not agree on certain family issues. Mrs. Will ran the family business and therefore worked very long hours. She openly announced the hardships she faced due to her increased work load, so that she could get more help from others.

Mrs. Wills: I do better now, but I used to scream and plead and fall apart. I used to get very annoyed if things weren't done when I'd ask someone to do them. I used to get mad, I used to say I am wasting energy.

Mr. Wills: No chance of sitting and watching TV, no not with that madam over there giving-off orders.

Six months after the interview, when I met with Mrs. Wills she had told me that she had a physical breakdown as a result of her business and family responsibilities.

Conclusions

Although couples' perceptions differed with regard to what constituted 'family order', they all tried to achieve it through a workable pattern in their household. The couples believed their hardships resulted mainly because of wife's participation in the labour market. Families under the Rigid model experienced household work conflict due to a lack of means to meet their unlimited ends. In addition to a lack of role bargaining, their internal or external commitments (such as higher household work standards, involvement in community projects, and upgrading their qualifications) led to several hardships. Although couples under this model were aware of their strengths and limitations, they still continued to struggle.

For example, for Mrs. Fields, under the Rigid model, 'family order' meant a spotless home, a three course meal, and a beautiful garden. It was a struggle to achieve all this because they both had full-time jobs and worked within traditional roles. On the other hand, the Brooms under the Trade-off model deliberately renegotiated their roles into a workable division, and lowered household work standards to avoid hardships. For them higher household work standards were not important in achieving family harmony.

A significant difference between the families under the two models can be observed from in the way in which they perceived and created family order (Table 8.1). In general, aspiring to a conventional family order meant also having a household work crisis. Families under the Rigid model experienced household work conflict frequently, and tried to justify their situation due to structural factors such as a lack of part-time job options, job inflexibility, traditional ideology, and a lack of adequate child-care facilities, all of which had a profound effect on desired goals. However, they did not attempt to make their life better by sharing household work. They accepted household work conflict as the price they had to pay for both being in paid work.

On the other hand, families under the Trade-off model who had renegotiated their work roles had settled for less, faced fewer household work crisis situations. For example, they deliberately reduced the wife's employment hours to increase the means for family activities. If the wife could not cope with her role overload then her husband took some chores off her hands permanently. Furthermore, they increased family resources through role sharing and reduced household work conflict. They also restructured their work and family demands so that they could avoid hardships. For example, the wife made a slow transition into the labour market by gradually increasing her paid work hours. In other cases, facilitated by a good communication and through role-bargaining, the couples had adopted an egalitarian division of labour even after having children.

9 Is the Style of Household Management Flexible or Rigid?

Now is the time to draw the strands together to show how and why some families managed household work contradictions effectively or ineffectively. I will do this by indicating a relationship between couples' interaction style and their household management strategies. Couples' interaction style bears on their ends and means, wives' dilemmas, gender ideology and role-relationships, as well as their perceptions of family order (Chapters 5 to 8). This results in particular strategies being devised and used in managing their three-job families. Conceptually, it can be claimed that 'if the style of management is flexible then household work strategies will be effective.'

Couples' style of household management mainly depended on how they perceived household work contradictions and how their perceptions impacted on their family order. The difference in the management style of families under the Trade-off model and the Rigid model can be found in the style of household management (rule 9 in Figure 3.3). Families under the Trade-off model used a flexible style that led to effective management of household work contradictions. In contrast, families under the Rigid model used an inflexible management style that led to chaos and ineffective handling of household work contradictions. In this book, a flexible management style is defined as one in which the couple works within an open and negotiable and somewhat egalitarian division of labour. A rigid management style, on the other hand, is defined as one in which the couple works within a gender-based division of labour with the wife reserving the right to call upon her husband and children for help.

By observing the relationship between family interaction style and coping strategies (Table 9.1) it can be claimed that families under the Trade-off model managed household work contradictions without much difficulty. In other words, if the family interaction style is flexible and hassle free and the couple uses long-term strategies, then the outcome is the effective management of household work contradictions. In contrast, if the family interaction style is rigid and full of conflict and the couple uses short-term strategies, then the outcome is the ineffective management of household work contradictions.

Table 9.1 Family Interaction Style and Coping Strategies

Family Model (No)	Family Name	Family Interaction Style	Coping Strategies
Trade-off (20)	Burton	-We priorities and settle daughter first (W&H)	-Mother helps, denial of social life to spend time with daughter
	Giles	-We have hired help to concentrate on family business (W)	-Hired help, discuss and solve problems on the spot, being in control
	Stone	-I have cut down on my work hours to be home when children come from school (W)	-Division of labour based on skill and time availability
	Knight	-We step into each other's roles easily (W&H)	-Husband regularly performs the evening child care chores
	Simmons	-We don't wait to be reminded (H) -We just do our chores (W)	-Following a strict routine, equal sharing, talking and listening to each other's work related problems
	Broom	-We share everything, we lived in a communal household (H) -We prefer loose roles (W)	-Sharing chores, lowered standards, no routine
	Faldo	-We share things (W&H)	-By reading the partner
	Long	-We keep on negotiating chores and keep a balance, fairness (W&H)	-Chore list, children help, giving each other a breathing space -Monitoring partner's mood
	Jenning	-He offers his help regularly (W)	-Husband helps, cutting corners
	Fielding	-I work to supplement income (W)	-Mother and husband help with child-care

	Harris	-I have to look for the baby sitter on my own (W)	-Husband helps by taking son away, patience
	Simpson	-Co-ordination, negotiation	-Flexible use of resources
	Donovan	-When I get the are you hungry question, I generally say no	-Cutting down her goals, negotiating hunger
	Sands	-She does everything even before I get here (H)	-Through total organisation, alerting each other
	Drummond	-I feel like doing the chores but it does not stay tidy (W)	-No routine, lowered standards
	James	-I do the chores with husband and children's help (W)	-Children help, physical culture classes -Skill based division of labour
Rigid (14)	Richards	-I manage with his help (W)	-Compromise and accept his way of doing chores, takeaways, organisation
	Short	-I am always planning (W) -I pay the children to do the chores (W) -I used to remind him to the point of nagging (W)	-Children help, do it on a need's basis, by planning ahead, postpone chores
	Kerrington	-She becomes the ring master (H)	-Children help, giving children more space and trying to understand their perspective
	Mason	-I stay up late to finish the chores (W)	-Some hired help, thinking ahead, staying up late to finish the chores
	Black	-He helps me when the kids are cranky (W) -I would ask can you do this?	-Neglecting chores, negotiating and stepping-out of traditional roles for children's sake, keeping the private separate from the public
	Ferguson	-We mainly worry about children	-Monitor the husband
	Davidson	-She calls for white tornado (H)	-Children help under instructions
	White	-I feel housework is my responsibility (W)	-Task postponement, some hired help, takeaways, everyone join-in to clean up
	Fields	-I think traditional system should still work (W) -I help her to keep peace (H)	-Task postponement, husband and children help, refuse social visitors

167

Hope	-I have to take others' help because I feel tired and stressed (W)	-Husband and children help, down play of her provider role
Turner	-I help her when she is stressed out (H)	-When the going gets tough the tough gets going
Turnbull	-I am not good at hiding and pretend everything is all right (W) -I tend to jump up and down when I am angry	-The housework is left until the week end, child care comes first
Brown	-I dump everything during the week to survive (W)	-Why battle just have a takeaway and you don't have to do the dishes
Wills	-I manage with some hired help (W)	-Children help, some hired help, hell with the housework, there is always tomorrow, everyone cooks a meal, priorities come first

With reference to rule 9 in Figure 3.3, this chapter specifies the nature and duration of household work management strategies negotiated and used by couples. The particular aims of this chapter are: 1) to ascertain families' management style, 2) to identify couples' interaction style, and 3) to describe strategies used by families in overcoming household work contradictions.

Trade-off families

Families under the Trade-off model were prepared to try different ways of managing their three-job households. They were willing to change their ends if their means were constrained. Similarly they stepped into each other's role if and when necessary and accepted each other's shortcomings. The wives in families under this model did not restrict themselves to family roles, they sought challenges outside the home in paid work. Children and their needs were given a higher priority over household work which gave the couples the satisfaction of having control over their three-job family situation.

Readjustment, communication and co-operation

'We had to cut back the social life' The Burtons were involved in full-

time employment and their two-year-old daughter had not yet settled with the baby sitter. They felt she was still very young for full-time substitute care. Because they were facing hardships in bringing up their daughter satisfactorily they minimised household work in order to spend more time with her. Mrs. Burton said: 'We try and prioritise because our daughter comes first. We tend to settle her first and then find things for us.' They had a skill-based division of labour and tried to reconsider family activities every now and then to accommodate their daughter's needs.

They tried to deal with their guilt by reducing contact with other people and increasing their time with their daughter. Mrs. Burton said: 'We had to cut back the social life and the running around trying to do too much and found we didn't have enough time for our daughter.' By cutting back their social circle they tried to increase their time spent together as a family. In addition, Mrs. Burton had arranged for her mother to come and mind their daughter in their own home so that she was not away at the baby sitter's for too long. This lessened her guilt because her daughter would be under the supervision of her own mother.

'It comes back to the communication and reading your partner'
Generally, the Knights managed their household work and family responsibilities through priorities and time availability. They believed they could only provide the best to their three boys if Mrs. Knight reduced her paid work hours to a manageable load. In this way she would be available to perform the family routines and keep her hand in paid work. They believed they had a 'good relationship' with each other that helped them through hardships.

> Mr. Knight: I guess everyone has a situation when it becomes too much and it also depends on the sort of day you have had. Sarah cooks and she seems to be there. If it is me that had a hard day then it might affect that evening if I was going to read to the kids or something then Sarah would step-in and vice-versa. If she has to go out or something then I would step into that role. The longer you live with somebody the more you read them.
>
> Mrs. Knight: The fact that we have a good relationship it helps to control stress.

Normally, the Giles had less worries about uncut grass or a basket full of ironing, because someone was paid to do these chores so that they could concentrate on the family business and children. In this way they had reorganised their household. Mrs. Giles said: 'I found that I have also become organised now that I am working than when I was at home.'

They coped with business-related stress successfully by making decisions 'on the spot'. They also tried to keep paid work and family life separate. The following accounts depict their stress management strategies.

> Mr. Giles: When I finish my job I would never bring work home. I believe what you can't do in eight hours you can't get that done at home. As soon as I walk through that door I will turn off from work.
> Mrs. Giles: Danny said to me the other day that we are best friends. I talk to Danny or talk to a friend. I can burst into tears or something. If something in particular is bothering you deal with them. Get it out in the open and be in control.

Being 'in control' was perceived essential to manage their busy lives effectively.

Usually, the Simmons followed a strict family routine through the week. Mrs. Simmons said: 'If I look at my housework past I can say we really have a routine and we just follow that routine.' Living just outside the town meant they had to rely on their own efforts for meals rather than on a takeaway service. Planning and following that plan strictly were perceived essential in keeping their household work under control. Mr. Simmons said: 'I like to plan things so that we know exactly what we are doing. I don't like a system where each one is hoping the other will do things.'

Their household division of labour was based on choice and fairness. They also had their own chores to perform so that neither was in the other's way. They coped with their paid work-related problems and frustration by talking and listening to each other. Mr. Simmons said: 'We talk about things and share our annoyances with other people. We communicate well'. They had a routine that was based on simplicity and equity so therefore neither complained nor bothered the other. They perceived household work objectively and did not make a fuss over its performance.

The Faldos were in a life stage in which there were not many demands from their children. They had more time and money now than ever before. Their teenage children were in many ways self sufficient. Their stress and pressures were paid work-related because they were both career-oriented and worked very hard. Mrs. Faldo said: 'It comes back to the communication, reading your partner.' They had good communication and therefore whenever one required 'time out' the other was there to relieve them.

> Mrs. Faldo: I am pretty lucky because when we do run into crisis in that I tend to run myself into ground a bit more. Barney (husband) is observant and knows when I am getting close to that stage he is quite capable of picking me up by the scruff of the neck and putting me to bed and making me stay there. If there is a housework crisis then everyone gets stuck in it. The children are very good that way in crisis.
>
> Mr. Faldo: In that situation either we will go and eat out or have a takeaway. If there is a mess in the kitchen then we tend to clean that up.

In difficult situations they worked as a team and managed their household and family responsibilities without much difficulty.

'I can't say if we aren't a team'   Mr. and Mrs. Jenning followed a preference based division of labour and faced household work hardships because of a lack of time and energy to meet the essential family activities. Mr. Jenning said: 'I think I have learned that one doesn't achieve anything by arguing. I guess it depends on what sort of 'compromises' we want to make with the 'ideals' we want to achieve.' Mrs. Jenning said: 'When we try to re-establish order in our house Garry is very supportive. It is pretty difficult when I come home and it's late and we haven't got anything to eat and the kids are ratty.' Being aware of his wife's inability to manage on her own he offers his help. The following interaction is an example of sharing chores during hard times.

> Mr. Jenning: Sometimes we cope and sometimes we don't.
>
> Mrs. Jenning: We are not too bad. I can't say if we aren't a team. I will ask you if you will do something. That's how its done like I would say could you do that and you often say to me, 'what can I do'?

'What can I do?' Meant delivering himself totally and passively into his wife's hands to help in household work. This also meant that she was not alone facing household work hardships. However, it also meant he was the person who delegated chores and took the responsibility of making sure the household work is done. Over the years Mr. Jenning had learned to appreciate his wife's desire for a 'clean and tidy' home. Although he had no qualms about doing the feminine chores during difficult times the overall responsibility of household management was left to his wife.

> Mrs. Jenning: Although Garry makes himself available it's now that he will recognise the 'gaps'. I think he wasn't able to see gaps or recognise mess particularly.
>
> Mr. Jenning: We don't want to contradict your responsibilities (laughs).

'I feel part-time is better' Mrs Stone had reduced her working hours to combine paid work and family needs. Now that she had a 'manageable' load she could organise the household as she desired. She had 'fitted' her job around their two children. Her 'being there' when children came from school was perceived to be very important.

> Mr. Stone: I am not sure if that is old fashioned but that's why Ann works part-time, to be there.

An untidy house did not bother them because they liked it to be homely, warm and comfortable. They had a division of labour based on skill and time availability, and every morning Mr. Stone helped his wife with breakfast and preparation of children's lunches. Mr. Stone tried to arrange his shifts in order to be with their children during school holidays. In this way Mrs. Stone could take over things in the afternoon when she finished paid work. Combining employment and family responsibilities was only possible by reducing her paid hours to part-time.

> Mrs. Stone: I feel having a taste of both worlds you could say part-time is better than working full-time. I could definitely say I am coping better. I mean I am home before the boys come back from school.

Mrs. Donovan had higher expectations of herself and her capabilities to care for the family and the household. However, when she found it was beyond her capacity to act like a 'superwoman' she had to rethink. She confessed: 'I used to have this stringent plan at the weekend as to what I wanted to achieve. I found that was not achievable so I cut down my goals.'

Under the normal circumstances they managed fairly well. However, there were occasions when things were too hectic, and as a result they had to figure out an easier way. The following example indicates the negotiations at meal-time.

> Mrs. Donovan: On a typical hectic day I'll say to you (looks at husband) are you hungry? Are you really hungry tonight? And he says no.
> Mr. Donovan: When I get the 'Are you hungry question', I generally say no.

'Are you hungry tonight?' Meant Mrs. Donovan was not willing to cook a proper meal for some reason. Her husband would understand her reluctance and would settle for a substitute 'improper' meal. Mrs. Donovan said: 'He is very easily pleased, I must admit and he'll say a toast and soup will do. Something quick and easy as long as it is something.'

The Simpsons constantly faced a number of hardships in running the household smoothly that required attention in several areas. Mrs. Simpson said: 'With us working full-time and having three children the household has to operate at a consistent rate.' Under normal circumstances they kept up with the household demands. They joined forces and strategically managed a number of tasks by paying someone to clean their house once a week and doing the laundry every night themselves. Mrs. Simpson said: 'We never have a basket full of ironing because we just keep prodding at it. Every night we have to do it, we work till 11 pm at night and we iron every day so it doesn't get accumulated and it never gets to a screaming mess.' A 'screaming mess' meant a lack of control and the inability to manage their household properly.

By constantly monitoring household work and keeping it to a manageable load they did not let things 'get out of hand'. They utilised resources at hand, e.g., having a takeaway, toast or a sandwich, and avoiding meal related-chores to catch up with other outstanding tasks. They were aware of their 'lowered standards' during the days Mrs. Simpson worked.

Mr. Simpson: She cooks better when she is not working.

Mrs. Simpson: We eat a lot better when I am not working.

Mr. Simpson: You say bugger the cooking and there is nothing in the fridge you go and have a takeaway.

Flexibility and negotiation in roles

'Our roles are not strict'   Mr. and Mrs. Broom avoided household work conflict by organising their household in such a way that they could avoid frequent household work crisis. Because they had three children, Mrs. Broom preferred to be employed only part-time. They preferred 'loose roles', but their friends and family tried to enforce the traditional norms and behaviour patterns in a subtle and sometimes not so subtle way.

Mrs Broom: There are women who don't like men doing the housework. When they walk in and Ken is doing the washing up you can see that they are a bit threatened. Like nothing is said up front but you know they are saying 'I don't look after him.' And if the house is in a mess then the women as well as men would judge that it is the woman who can't hold it together.

Mr. Broom: When we both come home from work and the lounge is a mess and the dining room is a mess it doesn't occur to me how the house is but Marian is more aware of that than me. I realised why it was because when people turned up and the things are messy then any criticism that comes back it is of Marian.

Because they had lived in a communal household where the household work was a shared arrangement rather than based on gender, they found it easier to deal with others' remarks and opinions. They preferred role flexibility so that they could cope better with paid and unpaid work. Mr. Broom said: 'Our roles are not strict and we decide then and there.' They also perceived their physical environment as 'casual', and therefore it did not require much detail while cleaning. Mr. Broom said: 'We are not living in a shaggy white pile carpet you know with plastered walls, where we have to take care of you know it is an old house.'

The Drummonds had been used to having the house to themselves before they had their daughter. Having a child in the house meant they had to redefine what constituted a family. Keeping the household 'clean

174

and tidy' became a chore that was not an issue in their childless years. Consequently, performance of household work was limited to only the essential chores for two reasons: lack of time and energy, and the 'short-lived' nature of clean and tidy homes. Mrs. Drummond said: 'The distressing part about housework is that it is destroyed five minutes later. It is very short-lived and I find a lack of control over the environment.'

Although she wanted to get up and pull everything out of the cupboard and have a 'big clean up' she was afraid it would not stay 'tidy' much longer. She admitted all she saw in her house was mess and found it 'dreadful'. In order to cope better they would have to stick to a 'routine'. This was not considered proper because their daughter was used to having a flexible routine in which she was fed and cared for on a needs basis: 'I think normal families do have a routine and I feel we should try and have one but that might add to our stress.' They were already facing hardships and wished not to constrain their lives further. Mr. Drummond said: 'No, I think we just go along how our daughter feels.'

Some families managed their households through a variety of strategies from devising a chore list to seeking their mother's help. The husbands under this model were willing to help their wives if and when required.

'It is a balance which we seem to negotiate quite often' Under normal circumstances, Mr. and Mrs. Long had a 'sense of fairness' about their contributions to household work. This was based on their perception of a 'balance' and 'fairness' that they wished to maintain in their marriage and family roles. Mr. Long said: 'Housework needs to be shared and I think in the end it is a balance. You know sharing to balance.' This balance was not a written contract based on rigid rules, but a vision in their minds as partners. Mrs. Long said: 'It's a balance which we seem to negotiate quite often. There are a few jobs that keep on changing around.' When one partner felt the other was getting bored and fed up with a monotonous chore then that chore was taken from them. If they had settled down to a particular routine and something disrupted it then they would have to renegotiate. They also had a 'chore list' stuck on refrigerator which monitored theirs' and their children's input in household work. The following accounts illustrate the fluidity of household management.

175

Mr. Long: Well if one gets sick of doing something then the other person can do it.

Mrs. Long: We have always shared housework but the balance is changing. There is no sort of 'cut and dry' world for people because if Dave has to travel then he is gone for a few weeks and that means I have to do everything. He has done the same like working as well as taking care of every household chore when I had gone overseas.

Also by keeping a 'close eye' on the other partner's mood they monitored paid work pressures and took extra household work to give them some breathing space. The following interaction is an example of their successful 'give and take'.

Mr. Long: This is what both of us do if one of us gets really crazy with work pressures and it is a sort of signal to us that things are going crazy and we will try to reorganise things.

Mrs. Long: Now that kids are old enough when things get really crazy they help.

Mr. Long: We give them more things to do or if she is marking papers then I will cook for two or three weeks or something.

With children's help Mr and Mrs Long were able to relieve each other from household work duties so that they could concentrate on their paid work commitments.

The Sands encountered a lower level of household work crisis, but faced job-related stress and pressures. Mrs. Sands was a nurse and worked on shifts. She wished for a more flexible routine so that she could fit her paid work around her family needs. While not on duty she tried to spend all her time with her son.

They also tried to make their home a comfortable place away from the rampages of the paid work place. Mrs Sands said: 'There is so much pressure at your work place you try to make your home environment very flexible.' By doing this they avoided any conflict, especially with regard to household work performance. Under the normal circumstances their household division of labour was fairly well mapped out. Mr. Sands said: 'It is not one or the other, black or white, whoever is more efficient in getting the housework done and who can have housework on their personal agenda.' However, some chores accumulated and caused concern. These chores were done by the person who was bothered about it.

Mr. Sands: Well Rene simply does most of the tasks that I simply don't do, they don't occur to me.

Mrs. Sands: Well it depends which task it is and who tends to avoid it. Mark does all the indoor cleaning like cob webs and things. It worries him, whereas it doesn't bother me. If he wants them done he can do it, and I know that he will do it.

Mr. Sands: Well I tend to do that. I don't like them, it is understood that I would do them.

This pattern made them responsible for some 'particular' chores. Although they felt it was not their own chore and it should not bother them they still 'alerted' the other. In this way they both checked one another to maintain some level of 'organisation' in the family.

Child-rearing hardships

'He called mum one day when he was having a hard time' With three children under five Mrs. Fielding had to find paid work to supplement their income. Mr. Fielding appreciated the fact that his wife assisted him in earning a living: 'Her skills came in handy and we are a little bit better off financially.'

Mrs. Fielding had worked out the expenses of child-care and decided against it because of its costs. They figured out it would be economical for them if Mr. Fielding cared for the children while she worked. Mr. Fielding found it very difficult to do this in his wife's absence. He said: 'I am here all day and I found it really hard to manage on my own. Now I have appreciated what she does. It is not an easy job and it's not a job that comes naturally to everyone, you have to work at it.' Mrs. Fielding related his frustration: 'He called mum one day when he was having a hard time. When I came back from work she said your husband has run away he has had enough.' Since she had been in paid work she had learned to tolerate lowered household work standards and disrupted meal-times and a certain amount of 'mess' all the time in their home.

'Just shut up and sit down while I eat' Mr. and Mrs. Harris faced some problems in their household mainly because they were still learning to be parents. They were coming to terms with the fact that their son was not a baby but a very active toddler. He often did not sleep during the day and therefore became cranky in the afternoons.

177

Mrs. Harris did not let him have his afternoon nap because he would stay up late at night. Somehow she was unable to establish a proper sleeping pattern for him. In the afternoons he wanted her whereas she needed to prepare his dinner. In these situations Mr. Harris either took over his wife's duties or took his son away so that his wife could do household work in peace.

In some situations the only way they coped was by having patience. However, their son tested them to their limits.

> Mrs. Harris: After settling him, you sit down to a meal and all of a sudden he gets bored and he wants to do things as well and you say 'Just shut up and sit down while I eat'.

'Our daughter had to take a day off school to look after her sick brother' Both Mr. and Mrs. James worked in full-time employment and had a skill-based division of labour. They faced difficulties in household work and child-care, especially during school holidays because they were both in nine-to-five jobs. Mr. James was a gardener, so his paid work load increased during summer. Consequently, during children's summer holidays they had to find substitute child care.

At the time of the interview they were finding it hard to get someone to care for their two children. Mrs. James could take time off but there were limits: 'I took a week off last week but I have to go to work tomorrow. I asked everybody, all our friends and all our kids' friends, everyone is going away this week.'

Another problem was during their children's sickness. Sending 'sick children' to school was not only considered morally wrong but also against school regulations. In situations when Mr. and Mrs. James could not find a substitute carer they had to leave their children on their own. The following accounts depict a strategy when all else fails.

> Mrs. James: Once our son was sick, I had a seminar to attend and Kenny had to be at work. Our daughter had to take a day off school to look after her sick brother.
>
> Mr. James: You see if your child is sick you don't want to send them to any one's house because you don't want them to catch the bug either. We find it very difficult.

Usually they managed household work by taking their two children's help. Mrs. James believed children should take part in household work: 'I think it is good for them in two ways. One is to realise that we are not here just to cater for them and the other is that it is a training for life.' She perceived two benefits from this: on the one hand they helped in the household work and on the other they spent time together as a family.

Rigid families

Families under this pattern worked within a gender-based division of labour and only some husbands willingly helped their wives. One can observe tension in their interaction style (Table 9.1), which led to the neglect or postponement of some chores. The wives also had to take the initiative to seek their husbands and children's help. In this way they waited to be pressured to help in the household work.

Household work crisis management strategies

'I will ring him at work to pick up some fish and chips'   Although the Richards had a gender-based division of labour sometimes Mr. Richards helped his wife in feminine chores. Invariably Mr. Richards offered to 'step-in' to help maintain control over their household routines. He said: 'If Nina was dependent on me and a full-time housewife, my expectations would be different. I wouldn't have to do any housework.'

In the morning Mrs. Richards often left the household 'as it was' and took care of it when she returned. Invariably she was held up at school or had to shop on the way home, or take the children to the local library. These demands took a valuable portion of time and delayed the household routines. It was then appropriate to buy takeaways and avoid cooking related chores. The following accounts depict the negotiation of takeaways.

> Mr. Richards: If we are in a stage when it becomes unbearable and we are desperate I might go and buy takeaways.
> Mrs. Richards: Yeah, I will ring him at work to pick up fish and chips or chicken and chips.

'Lately we have started to go to Pizza Hut'   Although Mr. Short believed in a traditional division of labour, he helped his wife because

she needed to be in employment to supplement family income. With three small children and Mrs. Short's evening shifts they decided to perform household work on a needs basis. Due to a lack of time they regularly postponed chores. However, a proper 'planning' of other household activities was essential to avoid 'conflict'.

> Mrs. Short: Well we will just sit down and talk about it. I am always planning things, what has to be done, make sure there is not going to be too much the next day for us, or it will just blow out.
>
> Mr. Short: I guess we get down to absolute priorities. Once that's done then other things are either negotiable or we leave them. When it comes down to meal and when we are both too tired to cook then we just might have cheese on toast or something. But lately we started to go to Pizza Hut which we haven't done before.

Mrs. Short tried to make her husband responsible for household maintenance: 'I used to remind him to the point of nagging and it was getting ridiculous. You know the more I nagged, the less he (husband) wanted to do it.' Unaware of how his wife felt about him he asked: 'What job is that?' Mrs. Short did not want to push the issue further: 'I would remind him to a point and if I feel that he won't fix them I would find how much it will cost us.' After finding out the cost of repairs she would negotiated with her husband. Mr. Short was obliged to perform the task in order to save money.

Figure 9.1 illustrates the negotiation of household work in three-job families. This figure is based on three-job couples' responses to the negotiation of family roles. Whereas the Rigid families negotiate household work by completing the entire negotiation process the Trade-off families go through only some phases.

In order to understand the process of household work negotiation one needs to picture a household in which both partners had returned from work and may have picked up their children from the child-care centre. Once they enter their family domain the following act takes place:

Phase one   The cycle starts with the wife taking charge of the unfinished household work left since morning. She gives 'subtle' hints to indicate the state of their household to which the husband responds by being 'unaware'. It is possible that the wife may exit the negotiation process to not to 'make a fuss' or by thinking that she would 'do it later'.

Phase two   It is a possibility that the wife feels strongly about the 'mess' and starts 'direct negotiation' by asking her husband for help. He shows 'reluctance' either by not taking any notice or deliberately ignoring her request (this happens as he watches TV or reads the newspaper).

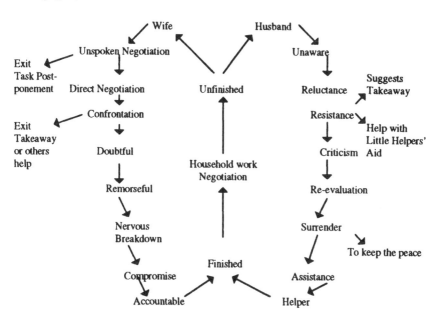

Figure 9.1
NEGOTIATION OF HOUSEHOLD WORK IN THREE-JOB FAMILIES

Phase three   Realising that she is not taken seriously by her husband she decides to take the matter a step further. Through 'confrontation' she attracts his attention to make him realise what 'needs' to be done in family's evening routine. He shows 'resistance' but suggests a 'takeaway' meal or rounds up children as 'little helpers' to 'tidy up'. She may accept the takeaway option or their help but this decision is based on how many times they have had a takeaway meal in the past week.

Phase four   If she doesn't opt out for takeaway meal and doesn't receive help from her husband then she feels 'doubtful' about her ability, as a wife and a mother, to hold the family together. Watching his wife in this state of mind the husband extends 'criticism' of her higher standards and 'justifies' his contribution by suggesting a takeaway meal. Although he finds a takeaway meal to be a good solution his wife feels bad for not providing a home cooked meal to her family.

Phase five   By now the wife has moved a step forward into the conflict and feels 'remorseful' about the whole situation. She either says nothing or gets 'verbal' as she frantically tries to do several tasks while dealing with her 'anger' and 'guilt'. On the other hand the husband begins to assess the situation through the process of 're-evaluation'.

Phase six   In the meanwhile the wife has had 'enough'. She 'looses control' and is beginning to have a 'nervous breakdown'. It is this state of affairs that makes the husband 'surrender' in order to 'keep peace'.

Phase seven   Once he pays attention and extends his help only then she beings to 'compromise'. He commits his 'assistance' and helps her.

Phase eight   In the process of initiating the negotiations and seeking help from her husband to deal with household work the wife confirms her 'accountable' role whereas the husband remains only a 'helper'. In this way the household work is finished until another similar situation takes place.

'In crisis situation we tend to put children first'   Mr. and Mrs. Black organised their household division of labour on the basis of time availability and interest. They strategically negotiated the procedural rules. The chores that one 'hated most' were delegated to the other partner. Mrs. Black said: 'I don't particularly like cleaning the shower so I am used to putting it off and Henry (husband) ends up doing it.' When a partner is 'talked into' doing a certain chore then that partner holds the 'right' to perform that task as he/she desired. In other words a partner 'gives up' the right to criticise the other when he/she has delegated a disliked task to the other partner. This mutual negotiation was an ongoing phenomena in their household.

Mr. Black described the extent to which he was prepared to put his time and energy to some monotonous chores: 'Between the two of us I guess I don't mind ironing. I will go and do the things we need for the next day and things like that. Because if they are not done then I would just go and do them. I am not particularly good at them but I'll do them and if I do them I'll do them my way.' Mrs. Black admitted: 'I don't make the beds everyday because that is not important and it is not going to hurt the children, but I usually keep this room tidy so I've got some place to show visitors.'

Apart from this usual pattern of coping the Blacks faced other problems, especially during evening meal time. They often coped with the evening routine by giving children what they liked to eat. Mr. Black said: 'You give them what they like to eat and they are happy. Even sandwiches, peanut butter and vegemite or something.' Mrs. Black confirmed this by describing the children as 'impatient': 'Usually they cannot wait that long, and they need to eat instantly.' They related a typical interaction during mealtime.

> Mrs. Black: Usually we just get in and do it. I do the cooking and in a crisis situation I would ask you can you do this? Take the kids, you can do this and that bit. Can you get the fire going? Can you feed the dog?
> Mr. Black: I'll peel the potatoes or bath the children and feed them.

By 'negotiating' and 'stepping out' of their typical roles they coped with their three children's needs fairly effectively during meals.

'She becomes the ring master'   Although normally indoor household work remained Mrs. Ferguson's responsibility, while her husband took interest in some indoor chores. The symbolic content of her husband's 'home-making' interest made Mrs. Ferguson somewhat anxious about her own responsibilities. She coped with this by 'turf-guarding' behaviour, i.e., by monitoring her husband's participation in the indoor chores. Under normal circumstances she wanted her husband to 'act' like a 'traditional' husband, but in the event of increased demands she called upon his help.

> Mrs. Ferguson: In crisis we tend to put the children first. It's like having a black out you calm them first and then get the candle. We make them comfortable, or feed them, or bath them, or put to bed or whatever.
> Mr. Ferguson: We mainly worry about the children. We first solve what they want to eat and then whatever is there we have it.

Apparently, if children's welfare was at stake they did not care 'who performs what chore' as long as it served the purpose.

The Kerringtons faced two types of conflict: a disagreement with their teenage children, and a lack of control over their household work. A conflict with their teenage children resulted from two aspects of parenting. The confusion was not whether to adopt a 'protector' or a 'guide' role but how to maintain a balance between the two.

They operated within a traditional pattern and experienced conflict during evening meals, especially when Mrs. Kerrington failed to plan ahead. In these situations they had their regular 'unconventional' meal. Mrs. Kerrington said: 'If the crisis is about the meals kids will eat something like a sandwich and if I am not tired then maybe cheese on toast or something.' Two of their three children were teenagers and were able to look after themselves. Mr. Kerrington said: 'Now they go out more often or have a take away or something.'

Generally, Mrs. Kerrington resumed the responsibility of keeping the family home in a reasonable order. She also kept on reminding the children to keep their rooms clean until the house reached a stage when she had to 'raise her voice'.

Mrs. Kerrington: When a situation like that comes I will make everyone know about it. I will make that very apparent.

Mr. Kerrington: She becomes the 'ring master.'

Mrs. Kerrington: I get angry and ask everyone to come and do it or help me. If I am really uptight and things are too much then (she clenched her fists) they do come and help me. After that things are normal again.

In the Mason household 'planning ahead' was perceived essential for meeting their household needs. Normally they coped with household work in a traditional division of labour, which was further strengthened by their individual skills. Although her husband helped around the house Mrs. Mason was conscious of the fact that she was responsible for housekeeping and therefore she had to be organised and efficient. They described a typical interaction.

Mr. Mason: If we are at a situation when the housework is not going to be finished then I will suggest we will attack it in the morning.

Mrs. Mason: I am not very good at that. I like to do that before I go to bed. Whereas he doesn't mind getting up in the morning and I don't like going to bed knowing I am not up-to-date.

Mr. Mason: And wake up really cranky.

Mrs. Mason: I'd rather stay cranky and get it done.

Similarly, the Davidsons had 'joined forces' when their house required cleaning up. Mrs. Davidson constantly observed the level of cleanliness: 'Every now and then I get upset when things begin to get too untidy and I will then announce 'white tornado' time and everyone pitches in.' They panicked when their visitors announced they were calling and the place was in a shambles. They called this strategy 'tornado time', which meant they required a joint action, facilitated by a shared understanding. Along with their three children they engaged in cleaning the house. The following interaction unfolds operation 'white tornado'.

Mr. Davidson: I will take on some work and eldest goes to another area. We all become very organised.

Mrs. Davidson: Yes, every body is allocated a certain area of responsibility and we all go and do that. I will say as soon as you have finished come back and I will give you another job.

This strategy was found to be highly successful in families that had teenagers. In a clean-up session everyone pooled their time and energy. During hardships an extra pair of hands proved very useful.

Some families faced household crises in cycles and coped temporarily. This was due to their rigid management style, which resulted from their mismanagement of ends and means, viriarchal division of labour, wives' never-ending dilemmas and an aspiration for a perfectionist family order.

The Wills household operated within a gender-based division of labour. They had two teenagers who were given set responsibilities. Normally they each cooked a meal once week days, but on Fridays they either had a takeaway or a slap-dash meal. A person who did not cook washed up. They had hired help for house cleaning and ironing which, Mrs. Wills considered a life saver: 'For $25 per week I get just about everything done, it is worth every penny. I could not cope otherwise if I didn't have that help.'

When things became unbearable they neglected the routine chores to perform only the essential ones. Feeding everybody was prioritised over doing household work. Mrs. Wills said: 'Well, priorities come first and if any one needs to be fed then the house is not important, hell with the house.' It was important for her serenity to have a good night's sleep. The household work was postponed because there was 'always tomorrow'.

Mrs. White described their household responsibilities in terms of who could actually stand a lower degree of mess, who was accountable for keeping the house tidy and who would feel guilty if her pupils saw their untidy home. Mrs. White believed it was her role to keep the household. Similarly her husband and children perceived household management as her main responsibility and therefore they very rarely initiated household work tasks.

As a wife and a mother, Mrs. White played a significant role in maintaining order in the family. In their household she was the one who declared the household situation to be 'out of control' and called upon others for help. She became verbal and told everyone that they would be cleaning up for the next half hour. However, she did not admit her inability to cope on her own.

Under normal circumstances they coped with their household work and family demands by using takeaway meals to avoid meal-related chores, by neglecting other chores, and by taking some hired help. Although her husband and children came to her rescue whenever she asked them, the household work remained her prime responsibility. The following interaction depicts a lack of commitment on others' part.

Mrs. White: Everybody does something to a varying degree depending upon how they felt. I would usually ask can you do the dishes or sweep the floor? And if you can't do it leave it.
Mr. White: Just leave it for a few days. Some things that don't fit the dishwasher they can sit around for a few days.
Mrs. White: Don't think exactly for a few days do we? (feeling a little embarrassed).
Mr. White: God so believe me.

Regaining control was perceived essential in maintaining family harmony and therefore the others 'gave in' to her demands.

Mrs. White: I yell and scream to get every body else to do it.
Mr. White: Yeah, tired and cranky and I can judge that. Either do it myself or go and buy it. I'd probably go and buy a takeaway or something it's

186

no big deal.

Similarly the Fields operated within a gender-based pattern and Mrs. Fields took help from her husband and children. Mrs. Fields believed that in their family an egalitarian household division of labour could not be openly negotiated: 'It is the way we are brought up and tend to think unconsciously that the father provide for the family and the mother should do the household work and look after the children.' However, interestingly, during hardships when she could not cope on her own then it was 'acceptable' for Mr. Fields to perform feminine chores - but only as a 'helper'. In other words, when she was unable to carry out the family routine due to her study commitments, fatigue, or children's homework demands, it was understood that they would 'step out' of their traditional roles and continue the family routine.

Mr. Fields would take over and resolve the situation through short-term strategies, for example, getting a takeaway so that their meal-related chores such as preparing, cooking, dish-washing and so on would be reduced. However, if the hardships were centred around children then they all became very 'co-operative'.

Mr. Fields: I guess I would organise because someone has to clean something, someone has to bath the youngest. Because you are doing something else, helping kids with the music or studies. It's not that I really take over, it's just...

Mrs. Fields: We would just become very co-operative in that both of us recognise that the other can't do a thing about it...so that person will take over.

By 'justifying' that they were not neglecting their children they felt their parenting standards were 'adequate'. This peace of mind was essential in maintaining their normal family atmosphere.

The Hopes followed a traditional division of labour. Mrs Hope said: 'I like to make sure that everything is all right and I do it properly and that's the way I like it to be.' On the days Mrs. Hope could not cope with the household work she relied on help from her husband and children. She reported that her inability to manage various responsibilities was mainly due to 'fatigue'. Under such circumstances children's help in household work became essential. The following accounts depict the strategic involvement of their children in household work.

> Mrs. Hope: Well if one has done more than others through the day that one gets to watch the TV and others will have to do their share. I feel if I ask them to do something they will have to do it. That is what teaching them discipline is about.

> Mr. Hope: That's what most kids don't do, respect authority...no respect at all. I think discipline is important, absolutely. Our daughter who is 12 helps...today she cleaned up, mopped the floor, did the bathroom...you see we have brought up our kids to help around the house...I think discipline is the answer.

The symbolic content of 'disciplining' children served two purposes. On the one hand Mrs. Hope received the needed help, and on the other hand it helped children integrate into the family.

'When the going gets tough, the tough gets going' The Turners faced problems as a result of their gender-based family roles. Normally Mrs. Turner managed, but any attempt to ask for help from her husband led to a conflict. She explained that any joint effort of managing family responsibilities was far from being a possibility. From the following accounts it is apparent that Mrs Turner managed household work on her own.

> Mr. Turner: I would chop the wood if it's got to be done then I'll do it. I might do the vacuum but don't ask me to do the bathroom or the toilet. If you are stressed out (which I am unaware of most of the time) or when you are not there I will start the tea and cook. As far as the household work is concerned it has to be left till the weekend.

> Mrs. Turner: When the going gets tough, the tough gets going.

Mr. Turner had become accustomed to a conflict over housework that had become a routine in their family.

On week days the Turnbulls coped with a lack of means by performing only the essential chores. Their three-year-old son and his needs were the most important activities on their schedule. No matter how tired or stressed they were they managed to bathe, feed, and read to their son regularly. They often postponed or neglected other things to fulfil his routine.

Mrs. Turnbull: Sometimes I'd just throw the hands up and say it's quite a life, we have to eat, Jason (son) has to be fed and sometimes bathed, the story has to be read and you work around that. It works out who has the greater need. Jason is the one that matters the most. The household work could be left until the end of the week.

Mr. Turnbull: He has to be in bed on a certain hour otherwise he becomes unbearable.

'Task postponement' was 'a way out' for them because they could not fit household work and child-care activities within their available means. Child-care needed time, patience, and energy. Although a lack of resources, inconvenience, and other constraints impinged on parenting, their effect was minimised by their values for designing parenting strategies. Child-rearing was not considered a chore that needed to be done, but a way to express love, care and nurture. By fitting other responsibilities around their son and his needs the Turnbulls did their best.

'Probably I did the bloody lot'   The Browns started their marriage within a traditional pattern. Mrs Brown had taken charge of the household before their children were born. Now that they have two jobs and two young children this has become questionable.

Mrs. Brown: I can't remember who did what...probably I did the bloody lot.

Mr. Brown: You did not.

Mrs. Brown: No we had the house cleaned...we had no kids and we had the money.

Normally, their household work load depended on whether it was a working-day or a weekend. During weekdays they barely managed and routinely 'left things till later', which meant they had to do the household work at the weekends.

Conclusions

Much of the variation in the coping styles of families was due to their ability to prioritise different activities. Children and related activities were a first priority in all families, whereas the rest of the household work was either neglected, postponed or minimised. Respondents' efforts of coming up with different ways of managing their three-job households reflected a continual desire to maintain order in their families.

The differences between families' coping styles can be observed from Table 9.1. Couples under the Rigid model operated within a gender-based division of labour, and wives faced anguish and frustration. Because they were solely responsible for household management they faced fatigue, anxiety and a lack of control. Consequently, the short-term coping strategies such as takeaway meals, task postponement, and a quick clean-up were negotiated on the spot in distress and conflict. Physical and ideological restrictions and a lack of time and energy led to a sense of uncertainty, which in turn hindered long-term planning. In other words, whatever strategy was designed had to be renegotiated when other unanticipated factors intervened.

In contrast, families under the Trade-off model faced household work conflict infrequently. They had long-term coping strategies, including role sharing, lowered household work standards, a reduction in wife's paid work hours. They also had either a rigid or a flexible household routine. They had restructured their household practices so that they had ample time and energy to fulfil other family responsibilities. Two strategies were found common: either a very 'strict routine' or 'no routine' at all. These strategies were long-term, which gave more security and stability to families. Because the conflict was infrequent and of a lower degree, the couples had a better sense of personal control over their households. Their deliberate restructuring of families also reflected their past experiences.

Although families under the Trade-off model faced similar structural constraints as families under the Rigid model, they coped better for two reasons. Firstly, the couples had unconventional ideals about what constituted a 'normal' family atmosphere. Secondly, they operated within a flexible division of household labour. Furthermore the couples had a shared agreement on household work responsibilities and its performance.

10 Managing Household Work Contradictions

In this book, I have sought to specify the rules by which three-job families managed household work contradictions whether effectively or ineffectively. As stated at the outset, I have argued *that in order to solve household work problems the families devise their own interaction orders. Household work contradictions can be effectively managed by means of devising specific sets of household management rules in the interaction order.* Household work contradictions take place as a result of the contrasting features in both the macro institutional order and the micro interaction order. An unequal division of household labour remains at the heart of this contradiction, as women take on the responsibility of running the family home in addition to their labour market involvement.

In Chapter 1, I assessed the increasing prevalence of household work contradictions in three-job families. It was argued that household work contradictions result from the contradicting features of the macro institutional order and the micro interaction order that cause problems for families in which both partners are involved in the labour market. I also discussed how household work has come to be defined as 'real work' (Oakley, 1974) and how it is different from the paid work. DeVault (1987) suggests that housework is a kind of family work that is organised differently from the labour market, and therefore it cannot be defined in terms of its most obvious mechanical parts. Recent research indicates that women do not enjoy the physical tasks of family work as ends in themselves (Komter, 1989; Shaw, 1988), but value them for interpersonal outcomes such as caring for loved ones (Hochschild, 1989; Thompson, 1991). Keeping in mind how women value family work it is understandable that they continue to fulfil responsibilities in the domestic sphere even when they are employed. As Mrs. Fields said:

'The absolute ideal thing is going to work and looking after children and not doing any housework'. So if household work contradictions are seen to be having adverse effects on family members, then wives and mothers are the ones who pay the price in terms of physical exhaustion and guilt.

In Chapter 2, I reviewed the relevant literature on how families seek solutions to the problem of household work contradictions. There is consensus that gender is socially constructed and therefore a household division of labour is based on socially constructed meanings of femininity and masculinity. Interactive theories discussed in this chapter described the processes and indicated a gender-based division of labour. In this chapter, I also argued the need for an articulated approach to study the household division of labour and the behind-the-scenes orchestration of family life.

In Chapter 3, I assembled a framework that addressed the contemporary debate on dualisms in sociology and made connections between the macro institutional and the micro interaction orders. This connection known as 'loose coupling' allowed me to envisage the relationship between the society and the family.

Chapter 4 specified in detail the methods used in the research discussed in this book. As the qualitative analysis proceeded, two patterns of household management styles emerged. The Trade-off and Rigid Models were idealised and defined and inserted into Figure 3.3 as part of the process of developing Grounded Theory.

In Chapter 3, it was claimed that the macro institutional order is loosely coupled with the workings of the micro interaction order (Figures 3.1-3.3). It was also contended that in practice in families this relationship can be seen as an absolute fusion. The substantive chapters (5-9) substantiate this claim by providing evidence and argument. From Figure 3.3 it can be claimed that the effective management of household work contradictions lies in the household management rules (5-9) devised by families in the Trade-off Model. In other words, if the rules are flexible and egalitarian in nature, then the family manages household work contradictions effectively. In contrast, if the rules are rigid and viriarchal in nature then the management of household work contradictions will be ineffective.

Chapter 5 elaborated the constraints experienced by couples in managing household work contradictions. In this book, a constraint was defined as 'a perceived hindrance of any type that negatively affected the performance of a three-job family.' The constraints were divided into two categories, resulting from both the macro institutional order and the micro interaction order. The main constraint experienced by families in both models was a lack of allocative resources: time, energy, and money (Figures 3.1-3.3), which limited the achievement of their goals. It was also observed that due to the influence of extra-situational resources: power, economy, viriarchy, and gender arrangements from the macro institutional order (Figures 3.1-3.3), the ultimate responsibility of managing the household fell on the wives.

Some wives had deliberately reorganised their life style so that they could manage paid and unpaid work effectively. They also renegotiated their goals in the light of available means. In contrast, other wives wished to achieve many ends (higher household work standards, good wife and mother image, career) with limited means. However, a lack of child-care was a common constraint that was experienced by families under both models. Those families who did not have extended family or close friends in the town were hard pressed for substitute child-care. Constraints pertaining to the macro institutional order such as inflexibility at paid work, gender ideology in the work place, a lack of part-time job option, and a lack of child-care close to the place of work, exacerbated household work contradictions-especially when husbands believed in and practised a traditional division of labour in the family interaction order (Figures 3.1-3.3).

The impact of household work contradictions described in Chapter 6 is about women's predicaments which result from their involvement in the labour force and their commitment to family responsibilities. These problems were a consequence of incompatibility between the macro institutional order and the micro interaction order (Figures 3.1-3.3). For example, aspects of the extra-situational resources-economy, job structure, viriarchy-in the macro institutional order were in conflict with the available allocative resources in the family interaction order. Similarly, aspects of general resources-typification, schema, cultural tradition-in the macro institutional order were in conflict with the motivational forces in the family interaction order. In this chapter, I have specified the ways in which wives handled their personal goals and role definitions in order to manage their dilemmas. Wives in all family types had to deal with identity issues as they constantly juggled paid work and motherhood. They wished to remain financially independent so that they did not have to ask their husbands' permission and money for little things such as getting a 'hair cut'. It appeared that wives with established careers faced fewer problems in terms of role conflict. They rationalised the need for full-time substitute child-care and the necessity to compromise household standards. They also derived satisfaction from being successful at paid work and considered their family roles to be important but not the only objective of life. Family roles were discussed in Chapter 7, where I explored whether couples renegotiated their household division of labour to manage household work contradictions. Although almost all couples agreed to the sharing of a provider role they expressed concern about the practicality issues, especially during child-bearing and child-rearing stages. They also believed that it was easier for women to give up paid work and rejoin the labour force later, because it was the 'normal' thing to do. These attitudes maybe a result of the ways in which the macro institutional arrangements such as viriarchy influence family members' behaviour in the micro interaction order. The implications of the macro institutional order are further evident as the wives' desire to be in part-time employment during child-bearing and child-rearing years was constrained. They found the job structure was such that they had no choice but to either be in full-time employment or give up paid work all together.

Some husbands who were liberal in their attitudes towards family roles renegotiated duties, so that the household chores were fairly equally divided. Much of role sharing was dependent upon the wife's willingness to relinquish control over the household. Even when the husbands actively participated in the household work the wives continued to take on the overall responsibility of running the household.

Household work contradictions affected three-job families in different ways. These contradictions were found to be present both within and between the macro institutional order and the micro interaction order. For example, within the macro institutional order aspects of extra-situational resources such as Equal Opportunity were contradicted by a lack of child-care and rigid job structures that mostly implicated women workers. Similarly in the micro interaction order the motivational forces were in contradiction with the images of self-other and family role relationships. In Chapter 8, I specified how household work contradictions impacted on the whole family: on husbands and wives individually and as a couple. The influence was judged on the basis of how they perceived the household work contradictions to be affecting their lives. If children were seen to be suffering then the situation was considered serious and consequently all energies were directed to make them comfortable. However, if the household work had to be neglected in the process it was considered as something trivial which could be taken care of in the near future. Every family's perception of family order was based on their socialisation, family values and the priorities which they maintained within the available resources.

The specific strategies of management of household work contradictions were described in Chapter 9. These strategies were devised as a result of contradictions within and between the macro institutional order and the micro interaction order that caused problems for three-job couples. Irrespective of their usefulness, the strategies appeared to be the outcome of the influence of both macro and micro orders (gender specific attitudes, viriarchy, traditional gender ideology, motivational forces, a lack of allocative resources). This substantiates the claim made in Chapter 3 in Figures 3.1-3.3 that in practice in families the relationship of the macro institutional order and the micro interaction order is an absolute fusion. Ineffective management (Figure 3.3) was a result of the short-term strategies used by families, who believed they were living 'one day at a time'. Strategies such as take away meals and task postponement were short-lived and caused much havoc in families and especially in the minds of wives. In contrast, carefully planned long-term strategies worked better and for longer periods.

Table 4.8 is a summary of the book and shows a dichotomous pattern in the distribution of Trade-off and Rigid Rules according to Family Patterns. The table was constructed on the basis of the nature of household management rules (Figure 3.3) employed by families. The general clustering of rules 5-9 under Trade-off and Rigid rules is consistent with effective management of household work contradictions (M) and ineffective management of household work contradictions (P) in Figure 3.3.

The ends and means of families under the Trade-off model and the Rigid model are different and contrasting in nature. Families under the Trade-off model have flexible ends and in this way they have increased their means through role sharing, lowered standards, and by sharing household responsibilities. In contrast, families under the Rigid model wish to achieve traditional ends. They have only limited means because of their viriarchal role ideology and traditional division of labour, and a desire to achieve higher household standards. In this way the main responsibility of household management is left with the wife.

Overall, it could be claimed that some families under the Trade-off model were capable of handling the household work contradictions. Their success was based on their commitment to make things work at home because both partners spent a great deal of time in employment. This required changes in the way they operated their households. They reworked their ends on the basis of available means, or in some cases renegotiated roles to increase resources. In other words, the husbands took on extra chores to reduce the actual time spent on household work by wives or the wives reduced their paid work hours. This gave the wives more time and physical energy to do other tasks. Although they did not deliberate on a particular set of household rules these emerged over a period of continual negotiation and renegotiation of a workable pattern.

The families under the Trade-off model succeeded in allowing the equity issues to filter through and deal with viriarchal constraints. This could be because of their unconventional ideology which gave rise to the Trade-off Rules (Figure 3.3). In contrast, families under the Rigid model allowed the macro institutional order constraints (viriarchy and traditional role ideology) to predominate their practices which could have been exacerbated by their own viriarchal role ideology. In other words, different household management rules also resulted from a difference in perceptions of the macro institutional order in three-job families.

From this it can be specified that the perceptions of families that employed household management rules under the Trade-off Model (Figure 3.3) were influenced by equality issues in the macro institutional order. In contrast, perceptions of families that adopted household management rules under the Rigid Model (Figure 3.3) were dominated by viriarchy. Other structural constraints (a lack of child-care, job structure, job inflexibility) equally impacted on the family interaction order. However, families devised several strategies to deal with these constraints, such as choosing to be employed part-time, deferring career ambitions, reducing social life to spend more time with their children, preferring takeaway meals to reduce household work (see Chapter 9). Other essential ingredients that facilitated effective management style were flexible gender ideology, a less constraining life stage and the willingness to 'make it happen' as a three-job family. Some of these characteristics can be found in Table 4.8.

196

Implications for theory

One theoretical increment in this book is in the graphical specification of the relationships between institutions and interactions. This specification in the conceptual framework overcomes the weaknesses inherent in symbolic interactionism, especially the conception of power. I used 'viriarchy', a masculine gender system, as an extra-situational resource in the macro institutional order to portray how men control women by virtue of being husbands. This form of dominance is practised by husbands through their control of the material means of subsistence for families, cultural representation of gender, and covert forms of discrimination practised in public contexts (Waters, 1989: 207) and in the relations of ruling (Smith, 1988:3). The notion of 'loose coupling' in Figures 3.1, consistent with Goffman's (1983) general view of the relations between the macro institutional order and the micro interaction order, draws selectively from different sources (Rawls, 1987; Sewell, 1992; Turner, 1987; Giddens, 1984) and provides a general claim. This conceptualisation was extended to Figures 3.2 and 3.3 to specify and demonstrate how couples handled constraints from both the macro institutional order and the micro interaction order.

The framework is generalised in Figure 3.1 and could be extended to other micro sociological analysis (everyday activities, practices and so on) and the larger scale, more impersonal macro phenomena like institutions and the distribution of power and resources. The specific claim (Figure 3.2) pertaining to family life could be used to study other familial interactions (socialisation, family crises, gender hierarchies, viriarchal power). The typological claim (Figure 3.3) could be used specifically as a conceptual framework to study the household management rules in three-job families within varied cultures. Overall, the notion of 'loose coupling' between the macro institutional order and the micro interaction order as developed, substantiated and argued in this book can be extended and/or modified to study macro-micro links in the context of other areas of study.

Another theoretical increment in the study is the specification in terms of posited rules 5-9. This is an advance over the more general and vague characterisations such as 'interaction' or 'mesostructure'.

It is also worth emphasising that there are contradictions between and within the macro institutional and the micro interaction orders. For example, in the labour market structural influences such as viriarchy,

197

gender arrangements and job structure are in contradiction with equity issues and affirmative action plans. Similarly in the interaction order the needs of self, role-relationships and gender ideology are in contradiction with allocative and authoritative resources. Thus, in studying social phenomena it is essential to conceptualise how these constraints contradict each other and how in turn they affect the daily lives of people.

Implications for practice

Household management rules under the Trade-off Model lead to effective management as assessed by the families themselves. The success is due to the nature of rules as the families judiciously handle constraints to achieve ends. They are also aware of role overload and dilemmas as the consequences of living in a three job family. Consequently they are prepared to renegotiate their roles and the ground rules of their household. Because both partners concern themselves about the smooth workings of their household they are vigilant for any impact on the family and on each other. They also choose to work within a flexible pattern so that they can step into each other's role should a need arise. They also design long-term but pliable strategies so that they are prepared for any contingency.

Even though the families under the Trade-off Model were coping with the third job, they were doing it at the cost of a normal family environment as they saw it. While they effectively managed household work contradictions they had to compromise on many desirable family activities, for example, individual and family leisure and recreation, more time with their children, higher household work standards, adequate sleep and a relaxed life style. In other words, effective management also required a reduction of family life (in the traditional sense) to an absolute minimum. On the other hand, families under the Rigid Model were caught up in the household work contradictions and often experienced both overt and covert conflict. This may have long-term implications for the couples' marital relationship and their relationship with their children.

There are also implications for future families. Children who experience the sharing of roles between their parents for the effective management of household work contradictions are more likely to be positive about family life and women's labour force participation. However, the same cannot be said for those whose parents struggle because of their ineffective household management rules.

There is a need for further research in this area. Perhaps it will be useful to conduct longitudinal studies on couples' quality of family life, careers, and organisational side of their lives according to the claims (Figures 3.1-3.3) made in Chapter 3. Researchers can conduct methodologically sound longitudinal studies to investigate which changes offer what types of benefits to employees and organisations alike.

The Australian government's commitment to the International Labour Organisation convention 156 and measures to enhance equality within the domestic sphere (Office for the Status of Women, 1992) are all steps towards equality between men and women. More positive changes in the family policy will encourage both men and women in adopting and practising egalitarian roles in the family. Perhaps Australia should consider a family policy similar to Sweden's (Swedish Institute, 1989: 4), where a total of 15 months of child-care leave is available for parents up to the child's eighth birthday. Some have even suggested shorter working hours (Bryson, 1993) as a positive step towards equal opportunity for parents to participate in their children's development. In this way, mothers will have the choice of staying in the labour market and increasing women's earning capacity. Equal earning capacity will then further increase women's choices.

However, structural or institutional changes are not enough. The study shows that the interaction order is a major source of innovation and adaptation. In support of this point, Table 4.1 shows no obvious structural correlates of Trade-off or Rigid patterns. Policy makers therefore need to consider how they can actually foster those family interactional processes which support equality, democracy and the rights of citizenship within the family itself. In other words, without making favourable changes in both the institutional and the interaction orders, contradictions will remain over the third-job of household work.

199

Bibliography

Able, E. K. and Nelson, N. K. (1990) *Circles of care: Work and identity in women's lives* (eds.) New York: State University of New York Press.

Angell, R. O. (1936) *The Family Encounters the Depression.* New York: Charles Scribner's Sons.

Arber, S. and Ginn, J. (1995) 'The mirage of gender equality: occupational success in the labour market and within marriage.' *British Journal of Sociology,* 59, 21-43.

Australian Bureau of Statistics (1983) *Cross Classified Characteristics of Persons and Dewellings.* Canberra: Commonwealth Government Printer.

Australian Bureau of Statistics (1996b) *Labour Force, Australia* Catalogue No. 6203.0. ABS, Canberra, January.

Backett, K. C. (1982) *Mothers and Fathers: A study of the Development and Negotiation of Parental Behaviour.* London: Verso.

Barrett, M. and McIntosh, M. (1982) *The Anti-social Family.* London: Verso.

Becker, H. (1953) 'Becoming a marihuana user.' *American Journal of Sociology,* 59, 232-42.

Beechey (1987) *Unequal Work.* London: Verso.

Berger, P. R. L. and Kellner, H. (1964) 'Marriage and the Construction of Reality', *Diogenes,* Summer, No. 46.

Berger, P. R. L. and Kellner, H. (1970) 'Marriage and the Construction of Reality' in *Recent Sociology No. 2.* H. P. Dreitzel (ed.). London: Collier Macmillan.

Berheide, C. W. (1984) 'Women's work in the home: Seems like old times.' In *Women in the Family: Two decades of change.* B. B. Hess and M. B. Sussman (eds.), pp. 37-55. New York: Haworth Press.

200

Berk, R. and Berk, S. (1979) *Labour and Leisure at Home*. California: Sage.

Berk, S. F. (1985) *The Gender Factory*. Plenum Press: New York.

Biernacki, P. and Waldorf, D. (1981) 'Snowball sampling: problems and techniques of chain referral sampling.' *Sociological Methods and Research*, 10, 141-163.

Bittman, M. (1991) *Juggling Time: How Australian Families Use Time*, Canberra. Office of the Status of Women, Department of the Prime Minister and Cabinet.

Bittman, M. and Lovejoy, F. (1991) *Domestic Power: Negotiating an Unequal Division of Labour Within a Framework of Equality*. Paper presented to Australian Sociological Association.

Bittman, M. and Lovejoy, F. (1993) 'Domestic power: negotiating an unequal division of labour within a framework of equality.' *Australian and New Zealand Journal of Sociology*, 29, 302-320.

Bittman, M. and Pixely, J. (1997) *The Double Life of the Family*. Allen and Unwin: NSW, Australia.

Blumer, H. (1953) 'Psychological import of the human group.' In *Group Relations at the Cross-roads*. M. Sherif and M. D. Wilson (eds.), pp 63-65. New York: Harper and Brothers.

Blumer, H. (1969) *Symbolic Interactionism: Perspectives and Methods*. New Jersey: Prentice-Hall.

Brennen, J. and Moss, P. (1991) *Managing Mothers: Dual Earner Households after Maternity Leave*. London: Unwin Hyman.

Broderson, A. (ed.) (1964) *Alfred Schutz: Collected Paper* Vol. 11. The Hague: Martinus Nijhoff.

Bryson, L. (1983) 'Women as welfare recipients: women, poverty and the state.' In *Women, Social Welfare and the State in Australia*. C. Baldock and B. Cass (eds.), pp. 213-223. Allen and Unwin, Sydney.

Bryson, L. (1993) 'Equality, parenting and policy making.' *Australian Journal of Marriage and Family*, 14, 66-75.

Burgess, E. W. (1926) 'The Family as a Unity of Interacting Personalities', *The Family*, 3-9.

Burgess, E. W. (1947) 'The family and sociological research.' *Social Forces*, 26, 1-6.

Burgess, R. G. (1984) *In the Field: An Introduction to Field Research*. London: Allen and Unwin.

201

Burgess, E. W., Locke, H. J., and Thomas, M. M. (1945) *The Family, From Institution to Companionship.* Third Edition. New York: American Book Company.

Colledge, M. (1991) 'Workforce barriers for sole mothers in Australia.' In *Sole Parents and Public Policy* (ed.), Reports and Proceedings of Social Policy Research Centre, No. 89. Kensington: University of NSW.

Collins, R. (1981) 'On the micro-foundations of macro-sociology.' *American Journal of Sociology.* 86, 984-1014.

Coltrane, S. (1989) 'Household labour and the routine production of gender.' *Social Problems,* 36, 473-490.

Coltrane, S. (1990) 'Birth timing and the division of labour in dual-earner families.' *Journal of Family Issues,* 11, 157-181.

Cooley, C. H. (1902) *Human Nature and the Social Order.* New York: Scribner.

Cooley, J. K. (1927) *Green March Black September: The Story of the Palestinian Arabs.* London: Frank Cass.

Corbin, M. (1971) 'Problems and procedures of interviewing.' In *Managers and Their Wives* . J. H. Pahl and R. E. Pahl (eds.). London: Allen Lane.

Coverman, S. (1985) 'Explaining husbands' participation in domestic labour.' *The Sociological Quarterly,* 26, 81-97.

Cronbach, L. J. and Mechl, P. E. (1955) 'Construct Validity in Psychological Tests'. *Psychological Bulletin 52, 4: 281-302.*

Denzin, N. K. (1989) *Interpretive Interactionism: Applied Social Research Methods Series* Vol. 16. Newbury Park: Sage.

DeVault, M. L. (1987) 'Doing housework: feeding and family life.' In *Family and Work.* M Gerstel and H. E. Gross (eds.), pp. 178-191. Philadelphia: Temple University Press.

Douglas, J. D. (1976) *Investigative Social Research.* Beverley Hills: Sage.

Douglas, J. D. (1985) *Creative Interviewing.* London: Sage Publication.

Douglas, J. D (1973) *Introduction to Sociology: Situations and Structures.* New York: Free press.

Evans, M. D. R. (1991) 'Working wives in Australia: influences of the life-cycle, education and feminist ideology. In *Australian Attitudes.* J. Kelly and C. Bean (eds.), pp. 147-159. Sydney: Allen & Unwin.

Farkas, G. (1976) 'Education, wage rates, and the division of labour between husband and wife.' *Journal of Marriage and the Family*, 9, 473-483.

Fielding, N. and Fielding, J. (1986) *Linking Data*. London: Sage.

Finch, J. (1984) 'It's great to have someone to talk to: the ethics and politics of interviewing women.' In *Social Researching: Policies, Problems and Practice*. C. Bell and H. Roberts (eds.), 70-87. London: RKP.

Finch, J. and Mason, J. (1993) *Negotiating Family Responsibilities*. London: Routledge.

Finch, J. and Mason, J. (1990) 'Decision taking in the fieldwork process: theoretical sampling and collaborative working.' In *Studies in qualitative methodology: Reflections on field experience* Vol. 2, R. G. Burgess (ed.), pp. 25-50. Greenwich: JAI.

Friedan, B. (1963) *The Feminist Mystique*. London: Victor Gollancz.

Game, A. and Pringle, R. (1983) *Gender at Work*. Sydney: Allen and Unwin.

Gauger, W. (1973) Household work: can we add it to the GNP? *Journal of Home Economics*, 10, 12-15.

Gavron, H. (1983) *The Captive Wife*. London: Routledge.

Geerken, M. and Gove, W. R. (1983) *At Home and at Work*. Sage: Beverley Hills.

Giddens, A. (1979) *Central Problems in Social Theory*. London: Macmillan.

Giddens, A. (1984) *The Constitution of Society*. Cambridge: Polity Press.

Giddens, A. (1987) *Social Theory and Modern Sociology*. Stanford: Stanford University.

Glaser, B. (1978) *Theoretical Sensitivity*. Mill Valley: Sociology Press.

Glaser, B. G. and Strauss, A. L. (1967) *The Discovery of Grounded Theory: Strategies for Qualitative Research*. London: Weidenfeld and Nicolson.

Glaser, B. G. and Strauss, A. L. (1968) *Time for Dying*. Chicago: Aldine.

Goffman, E. (1959) *The Presentation of Self in Everyday Life*. New York: Doubleday Anchor.

Goffman, E. (1967) *Interaction Ritual*. Garden City: Double Day.

Goffman, E. (1983) 'The interaction order.' *American Sociological Review*, 48, 1-17.

Goldin, C. and Thomas, J. (1984) 'The co-operative model in correctional education: symbol and substance?' *Adult Education Quarterly*, 34, 123-134.

Goodnow, J. J. and Bowes, J. M. (1994) *Men, Women and Household Work*. Melbourne: Oxford Press.

Habermas, J. (1982) 'Reply to my critics.' In *Habermas: Critical Debates*. J. Thompson and J. Held (eds.), pp. 219-283. Basingstoke: Macmillan.

Handel, G. (ed.) (1968) *Psychosocial Interior of the Family*. London: Allen and Unwin.

Hardyck, C. and Petrinovich, L. F. (1975) *Understanding Research in the Social Sciences*. London: Saunders Company.

Harper, J. and Richards, L. (1986) *Mothers and Working Mothers*, second ed. Melbourne: Penguin.

Hays, S. (1994) 'Structure and agency and the sticky problem of culture.' *Sociological Theory*, 12, 57-71.

Heiss, J. (ed.) (1968) *Family Roles and Interaction*. London: Allen and Unwin.

Hertz, R. (1986) *More equal than others: Women and men in dual-career marriages*. Berkeley: University of California Press.

Hess, R. D. and Handel, G. (1968) 'The Family as a Psychosocial Organisation'. In *The Psychosocial Interior of the Family*. G. Handel (ed.), pp. London: Allen and Unwin.

Hill, M. S. (1985) 'Investments of time in houses and durables.' In *Time, Goods and Well-being*. F. T. Juster and F. P. Stafford (eds.). Institute for Social Research: Ann Arbor.

Hochschild, A. with Machung, A. (1989) *The Second Shift*. New York: Viking.

Holmstrom, E. (1985) *Women's Time, Men's Time, What We Say and What We Do*. Paper presented to Australian and New Zealand Association for the Advancement of Science Conference, Monash University, 26-30 August.

Hood, J. (1983) *Becoming a Two Job Family*. New York: Praeger.

Huber, J. and Spitz, G. (1983) *Sex Stratification: Children, Housework and Jobs*. New York: Academic Press.

Jary, D. and Jary, L. (1991) *Collins Dictionary of Sociology*. Harper Collins: Glasgow.

Kellaher, L. Peace, S. and Willcocks, D. (1990) 'Triangulating data.' In *Researching Social Gerontology: Concepts, Methods, And Issues*, S. Peace (ed.), pp, 115-128. London: Sage.

Kirk, J. and Miller, M. L. (1990) *Reliability and Validity in Qualitative Research*. California: Sage.

Komter, A. (1989) 'Hidden power in marriage.' *Gender and Society*, 3, 187-216.

LaRossa, R and D. C. Reitzes. (1993) 'Symbolic interactionism and family studies.' In *Sourcebook of Family Theories and Methods: A conceptual approach*. P. G. Boss, W. J. Doherty, R. LaRossa, W. R. Schumm, and S. K. Steinmetz (eds.), pp. 135-163. New York: Plenum Press.

Layder, D. (1993) *New Strategies in Social Research*. Cambridge: Polity Press.

Layder, D. (1994) *Understanding Social Theory*. London: Sage.

Lein, L. (1984) *Families without Villains*. Toronto: Lexington Books.

Lengermann, P. M. and G. Niebrugge-Brantley (1992) 'Contemporary Feminist Thought' In *Contemporary Sociological Theory*. G. Ritzer (ed.), pp 309-359. New York: McGraw-Hill inc.

Lofland, J. and Lofland, H. (1984) *Analysing Social Settings*. Belmont: Wadsworth.

Lopata, H. Z. (1971) *Occupation: Housewife*. London: Oxford University Press.

Luxton, M. (1980) *More than a Labour of Love*. Toronto: Women's Press.

Maines, D. R. (1982) 'In search of mesostructure: studies in the negotiated order.' *Urban Life*, 11, 267-279.

Mann, P. (1988) 'Personal Identity Matters. *Social Theory and Practice*, 14, 285-317.

McCall, G. J. and J. L. Simmons (1969) *Issues in Participant Observation*. Reading: Addison-Wesley.

Mederer, H. J. (1993) 'Division of labour in two-earner homes: task accomplishment versus household management as critical variables in perceptions about family work.' *Journal of Marriage and the Family*, 55, 133-145.

Meltzer, B. N., Petras, J. W., and Reynolds, L. T. (1975) *Symbolic Interactionism: Genesis, Varieties, and Criticism*. London: Routledge and Kegan Paul Ltd.

Morgan, D. J. H. (1981) 'Men, masculinity and the process of sociological inquiry.' In *Doing Feminist Research*. H. Roberts (ed.), pp. 83-113. London: RKP.

O'Donnell, C. and Hall, P. (1988) *Getting Equal*. Sydney: Allen and Unwin.

Oakley, A. (1974) *The Sociology of Housework*. Oxford: Blackwell.

Oakley, A. (1981) 'Interviewing women: a contradiction in terms.' In *Doing Feminist Research*. H Robert (ed.), pp. 30-61. London: RKP.

Office for the Status of Women, Department of Prime Minister and Cabinet (1992) *Working Families: Sharing the Load: An Issue Kit for the Workers with Family Responsibilities Program*. Canberra: AGPS.

Pahl, R. E. (1984) *Divisions of Labour*. Oxford: Basil Blackwell.

Pestello, F. and Voydanoff, P. (1991) 'In search of mesostructure in the family: an interactionist approach to division of labour.' *Symbolic Interaction*, 14, 105-128.

Piotrkowski, C. (1979) *Work and the Family System*. New York: The Free Press.

Pleck, J. H. (1985) *Working wives/working Husbands*. Beverley Hills: Sage.

Potuchek, J. L. (1992) 'Employed wives' orientations to breadwinning: a gender theory analysis.' *Journal of Marriage and the Family*, 54, 548-558.

Presland, P. and Antill, J. (1987) 'Household division of labour: the impact of hours worked in paid employment.' *Australian Journal of Psychology*, 39, 273-291.

Rawls, A. (1987) 'The interaction order sui generis: Goffman's contribution to social theory.' *Social Theory*, 5, 136-49.

Richards, L. (1985) *Having Families*. Victoria: Penguin.

Rock, P. (1979) *The Making of Symbolic Interactionism*. London: Macmillan.

Ross, C. (1987) 'The division of labour at home.' *Social Forces*, 65, 816-833.

Rubin, I. S. (1979) 'Retrenchment, loose structure and adaptability in the university.' *Sociology of Education*, 52, 211-222.

Russell, G. (1983) *The Changing Role of Fathers?* St. Lucia: University of Queensland Press.

Sewell, Jr. W. H. (1992) 'A theory of structure: duality, agency, and transformation.' *American Journal of Sociology*, 98, 1-29.

Sharpe, S. (1984) *Double Identity: The Lives of Working Mothers.* London: Penguin.

Shaw, E. and Burns, A. (1993) 'Guilt and the working parent.' *Australian Journal of Marriage and the Family*, 14, 30-43.

Shaw, S. M. (1988) 'Gender differences in the definition and perception of household labour.' *Family Relations*, 37, 333-337.

Shelton, B. A. (1992) *Women, Men and Time: Gender Differences in Paid Work, Housework and Leisure.* Cambridge: Greenwood.

Smith, D. (1979) 'A sociology for women.' In *The Prism of Sex.* J. Sherman, and E. Beck (eds.), pp. 135-187. Madison: University of Wisconsin Press.

Smith, D. (1988) *Everyday World as Problematic.* Milton Keynes: Open University Press.

Stacy, M. (1981) 'The Division of Labour Revisited or overcoming the two Adams', In *Practice and Progress: British Sociology 1950-80.* P. Abrahms, R. Deem, J. Finch and P. Rock (eds.) London: Allen and Unwin.

Stafford, R., Backman, E., and Dibona, P. (1977) 'The division of labour between cohabiting and married couples.' *Journal of Marriage and the Family*, 39, 43-57.

Strauss, A. (1978) 'A social world perspective.' In *Studies in Symbolic Interaction* Vol. 1. Denzin, N. (ed.), New York: Jai Press.

Strauss, A. (1978) *Negotiations: Varieties, Contexts, Processes, and Social Order.* London: Jossey-Bass.

Strauss, A. (1987) *Qualitative Analysis for Social Scientists.* New York: Cambridge University Press.

Strauss, A. and J. Corbin (1990) *Basics of Qualitative Research, Grounded Theory Procedures and Techniques.* London: Sage.

Strauss, A., Schatzman, L., Ehrlich, D., Butcher, R., and Sabshin, M. (1973) 'The hospital and its negotiated order.' In *People and Organisations.* G. Salaman and K. Thompson (eds.), pp. 303-20. London: Longman.

Swedish Institute (1989) *Facts Sheets On Sweden: Equality Between Men and Women.* Stockholm, September.

Szalai, A. (1972) *The Use of Time. Daily Activities of Urban and Suburban Populations in Twelve Countries.* (ed.) Paris: Mouton.

Thomas, J. (1984) 'Some aspects of negotiated order, loose coupling and mesostructure in maximum security prisons.' *Symbolic Interaction*, 7, 213-231.

Thompson, L. (1991) 'Family work: women's sense of fairness.' *Journal of family Issues*, 12, 181-196.

Thompson, L. and Walker, A. J. (1989) 'Gender in families: women and men in marriage, work and parenthood.' *Journal of marriage and the Family*, 51, 845-872.

Turner, J. H. (1987) 'Toward a sociological theory of motivation.' *American Sociological Review*, 52, 15-27.

Turner, R. H. (1962) 'Role-taking: process versus conformity.' In *Human Behaviour and Social Processes.* Rose, A. M. (ed.), pp. 20-40. Boston: Houghton-Miffin.

Vanek, J. (1980) 'Time spent in housework.' In *The Economics of Women and Work.* Amsden, A. (ed.), pp. 82-90. New York: Penguin.

Walker, K. and Woods, M. (1976) *Time Use: A Measure of Household Production of Family Goods and services.* Washington: Centre for the Family of the Home Economic Association.

Waters, M. (1989) 'Patriarchy and Viriarchy: an exploration and reconstruction of concepts of masculine domination.' *Sociology* 23, 1171-89.

West, C. and Zimmerman, D. (1987) 'Doing gender.' *Gender and Society*, 1, 125-51.

Wiley, N. (1988) 'The micro-macro problem in social theory.' *Sociological Theory*, 6, 254-61.

Winter, W. D. and Ferreira, A (eds.) 1969 *Research in Family Interaction.* California: Palo Alto.

Women's Bureau, Department of Labour and National Service (1968) *Women and the Workforce No. 6: Facts and Figures.* Government Printer.

Women's Bureau, Department of Employment, Education and Training (1990) *Women and Work.* Spring, DEET. Canberra.

Wynne, L. C., Ryckoff, I. M. Day. J. and Hirsh, S. I. (1967) 'Pseudo-mutuality in the Family Relations of Schizophrenics' in *The Psychosocial Interior of the Family: A Sourcebook for the Study of Whole Families*. G. Handel (ed.), pp. 443-65. Chicago: Aldine.

Yeandle, S. (1984) *Women's Working Lives*. London: Tavistock.

Index

—B—

Benefits of paid work for women,
107

—C—

Child-care responsibilities, 81
Child-rearing hardships, 209
Communication between
husbands and wives, 142
Conceptual framework, 39
general claim, 40
specific claim, 43
typological claim, 46
Conflicting images and needs of
women, 110
constraint, 68
contradictions. See also household
work contradictions

—D—

dualism, 7, 31, 32, 34, 36, 38, 39
feminism's position on, 32
Giddens's position on, 34
in social theory, 31

—E—

Employed mothers' guilt, 101
Employed women and economic
independence, 103
Employed women and financial
independence, 120

—F—

family models, 63

Rigid Model, 7, 46, 48, 74,
235, 237
Trade-off model, 124, 166,
167, 168, 174, 183, 193,
195, 201, 224, 229, 230
family order, 82, 168, 183, 193,
195, 219, 229
Flexibility and negotiation in
roles, 206
flexible management style, 195
Frustration and household work
crisis, 178

—H—

Hardships of three-job families,
88
household management
as a job, 11
Household management
strategies, 144
household work, 6
changing perceptions, 16
increasing contradictions, 13
household work contradictions, 7,
12, 16, 19, 20, 26, 28, 29, 30,
31, 45, 46, 48, 49, 50, 51, 59,
63, 64, 67, 68, 124, 168, 179,
195, 200, 225, 226, 227, 228,
229, 237
Household work crisis
management strategies, 212

—I—

Implications for practice, 236
Implications for theory, 235
inflexible management style, 195

interaction order, 38

—K—

knowledgeability, 36

—L—

Lack of adequate child-care, 79
Lack of part-time job option for
    women, 74
Lack of permanent employment
    for women, 86
lower level of mess, 154

—M—

mesostructure, 37
methods
    symbolic interactionist, 49

—N—

Nature of household work, 76
Negotiated order, 37, 40
Negotiation of roles, 148

—P—

Patriarchal ideology, 32
Planning and assessment of
    priorities, 174
pseudomutuality
    in domestic division of labour,
    11

—R—

Reaction to household work crisis,
    185
Readjustment, communication
    and co-operation, 201
research process
    analysis, 63
    exploration

participation observation,
    59
families interviewed, 54
inspection
    intensive interviewing, 61
recording and transcription, 62
research techniques, 58
selection of families, 52
resources
    allocative, 35
    authoritative, 40
    extra-situational, 227
    general, 38, 45, 227
    lack of resources, 82
Rigid families, 67
role-making, 34
role-overload, 95
rules, 35

—S—

screaming mess, 206
short-term coping strategies, 224
Strategies and Tactics, 21
structure, 31, 35

—T—

the third job, 6, 13. See also
    household work
Trade-off families, 67
Traditional division of labour,
    151
Traditional family order, 183

—V—

Validity, 50
viriarchy, 39, 46, 68, 227, 229,
    230, 235, 236

—W—

white tornado, 199, 233

211

For Product Safety Concerns and Information please contact our EU
representative GPSR@taylorandfrancis.com Taylor & Francis Verlag GmbH,
Kaufingerstraße 24, 80331 München, Germany

Printed and bound by CPI Group (UK) Ltd, Croydon, CR0 4YY
08/05/2025
01864370-0001